THE
Confederate States of America
IN PROPHECY

BY

THE REV. W. H. SEAT
OF THE TEXAS CONFERENCE

Southern Methodist Episcopal Church

Nashville, Tenn.

edited by
Dr. William G. Peters

CHATTANOOGA
C. S. Printing Office
2014

Originally published in Nashville, A.D. 1861, by the Southern Methodist Publishing House, in the CONFEDERATE STATES OF AMERICA.

Copyright © 2014, Dr. William G. Peters, President, THE CONFEDERATE STATES OF AMERICA, INC. — All rights reserved in all media formats under Berne Convention for U.S. and International Copyrights.

Published by the CONFEDERATE STATES PRINTING OFFICE[1], CONFEDERATE STATES OF AMERICA, INC.

---

[1] A division of the Confederate States of America, Inc. Also designated the C.S. PRINTING OFFICE.

Contents

FOREWORD i

PREFACE iii

CHAPTER I — THE FOUR GREAT MONARCHIES

Babylonian empire—Medeo-Persian empire—Grecian or Macedonian empire—Roman empire—Ten toes and ten horns—Little horn—Iron and clay—Reconstruction of the Roman empire. 1

CHAPTER II — The United States

The closing symbols in the visions agree—The mountain with the Ancient of days—The stone with the one like the Son of man—The text—Bishop Newton—Civil governments—Tenor of the visions—Necessities of the case—The Ancient of days not God in person, in nature, in revelation, in providence, but in government—Stone not the Church—Date—Baldwin—Conflict with despotism; from without; sudden—Takes the place of the despotism it destroys—Called a "kingdom"—Dr. Clarke's exposition—Dr. Baldwin's—Harmony of the visions 11

CHAPTER III — The United States — Continued

The mountain and the ancient identified with the mountain of the Lord's house, or Israel restored—The typical system—The church—The state—Israel restored not spiritually—not literally—but in the antitype. 23

CHAPTER IV — The United States — Continued

The Fifth Kingdom the United States—Proofs presumptive and direct—United States probably in prophecy—Her extent, growth, power, a Free Nationality—Date of the Fifth Power—Judges—The Little Horn—Outside the Roman Empire. 31

CHAPTER V — THE CONFEDERATE STATES

The closing symbols represent the Confederate States —The stone cut out of the mountain—without hands—Isa. 66:7-8.—Isa. 4.—The mountain of the house of the Lord—The trouble of Zion —The seven women—Micah 4, 5.—The mountain of the house—The remnant—The first dominion—The birth of the Savior—Birth of the man child—Seven shepherds, and eight principal men—The war. ...47

CHAPTER VI — The Confederate States — Continued

Zechariah's prophecies—Division of the Union—Border States as the slain shepherds—The eleven states as "the third"—The divided mountain—Ezek. 34. —The gathered flock judged and divided—Isa. 65:11-16—The Northern army—The American flag—Division—Contrast—One like the Son of man—Character of the government—How established—When it appears. 65

The Conclusion

Philosophy of our theory—The book of Revelation—The time of trouble—Convulsions in Europe—Fall of the United States—The present war—Five months—Our national fast—Battle of Manassas—Breaking the blockade—National resurrection—The millennium—The final judgment—Heaven. 79

Foreword

The secession of the Southern States to form a new country, THE CONFEDERATE STATES OF AMERICA, was a time of joy and jubilation to be free from the grasping spirit of puritan New England Yankees.

The Confederacy was formed in peace, and began its existence without opposition from the United States Government as President James Buchanan rightly understood that the States, as ratifiers of the Constitution, had the right to leave just as much as to join the federal compact.

Lincoln, however, was determined to force the Southern States back into the Union. Rejecting all peace overtures by the Confederacy, Lincoln raised an army for this purpose, and caused the war to begin.

In its exuberance the Confederate citizenry rushed to the colors, and fielded the greatest citizen army the world has ever seen.

As the young nation, and a Christian nation at that, began its struggle to preserve its independence, many began to look at scripture and history to bolster the nation in its fight against Yankee tyranny. This work, by Rev. W. H. Seat, a Southern Methodist minister, is part of this philosophical and religious effort.

The work is a bit odd in that it posits a secular new Israel as fulfillment of Daniel's vision. The United States is the secular Israel, and the Confederate States the secular restored Judah.

This book is printed as a part of our series of works published during the brief period of freedom of the Confederate States, before our continuing occupation by the Yankee government.

In many ways this work appears to be an extension of the work of the Rev. F.E. Pitts of Nashville, Tennessee later entitled *The U.S.A. in Bible Prophecy*. Of what church he was affiliated with we do not know, although possibly Methodist, as his book had an ad at the back for Methodist materials. If so, he was perhaps Rev. Seat's colleague.

Rev. Pitts preached his sermon - *A Defence of Armageddon or Our Great Country Foretold in the Holy Scriptures* - to the U.S. Congress in the Capitol building on Washington's birthday in 1857.

In it he identifies the United States as the 5th Government of the prophet Daniel - the stone cut from the mountain. Rev. Seat continues from this point, in his exposition that the CONFEDERATE STATES are the little stone cut from this big stone.

This eschatology of the United States and the CONFEDERATE STATES were a part of the idea that these were countries special to God, each with its mission to play.

Obviously, the Confederacy was conquered and occupied; nevertheless it lives on in memory and legality as the government never surrendered.

DEO VINDICE!

Dr. William G. Peters
President
THE CONFEDERATE STATES OF AMERICA, INC.
Anno Domini 2014

Preface

THIS little book contains no adequate discussion of the subject of which it treats, but rather an exposition of the grand prophetic visions recorded in Dan. 2 and 7, as corroborated and explained by other prophecies of the Old Testament Scriptures.

Our object has been, in discoursing and lecturing during a hurried and laborious tour through the Confederate States, and is now, in the publication of this little work, to call attention to the subject, and, if not to convince, at least induce a more careful examination of the prophecies, and prepare the mind for such manifestations of the truth, as Providence may furnish in the events of the future.

It may be thought that too much space is occupied with the United States in prophecy; but there is such an intimate connection between the fifth and sixth symbols in the visions, as to render the clear identification of the fifth essential.

It is hardly necessary to acknowledge indebtedness to Dr. Baldwin, as to this dement, in view of the references quotations from his book, to be found in the discussion itself, though we have endeavored to extend and strengthen the argument.

We differ with him, as the reader will see, in the application of the symbols. We have endeavored to show that the United States were not only "the Ancient of days," but also "the mountain." When this is fully made out, the identification of the Confederate States as the sixth power, or the stone cut out of the mountain, is easy, and even necessary.

The book is given to the public, not because an ingenious theory could be framed suitable to the prejudices and wishes of our people, but because we believe these things to be true, and that if true they ought to be understood.

The work has been, under the pressure of circumstances, hastily written and passed through the press, and is not as thorough in some of its discussions, or as perspicuous in style, as could be desired. For its blemishes and defects, the reader's indulgence is craved. It is given to the public with the earnest prayer that the Divine blessing may be upon it, as an humble attempt to unfold his providence and his Word.

Nashville, October 1, 1861.

THE
Confederate States in Prophecy

CHAPTER I
THE FOUR GREAT MONARCHIES.

Babylonian empire—Medeo-Persian empire—Grecian or Macedonian empire—Roman empire—Ten toes and ten horns—Little horn—Iron and clay—Reconstruction of the Roman empire.

THE vision of Nebuchadnezzar, and the first of Daniel's visions, recorded respectively in the second and seventh chapters of the book of Daniel, furnish, it is believed, the key to the leading national and political prophecies, both of the Old and New Testament Scriptures.

The identity in meaning of these 'visions' is entirely apparent. Dr. Clarke says of the first vision of Daniel, "This dream is the same in meaning, under different emblems, as that of Nebuchadnezzar's metallic image; but in Daniel's dream several circumstances are added." Scott also declares, "It contains for substance the prophetical intimations of Nebuchadnezzar's dream, but under different allusions, and with many additional circumstances."

Bishop Newton says, "What was revealed unto Nebuchadnezzar in the second year of his reign concerning the four great empires of the world, was again revealed unto Daniel (chap. 7.) with some enlargements and additions, in the first year of Belshazzar, that is, about eight and forty years afterwards." This identity will more fully appear as we proceed in the investigation.

We invite attention to these four great successive empires, in the order in which they appear in the visions. In Nebuchadnezzar's vision they are represented as a great metallic image, consisting of four sections; in Daniel's vision, as four successive beasts.

I. THE BABYLONIAN OR CHALDEAN EMPIRE.

The description is thus: "This image's head was of fine gold." (2: 32.) "The first (beast) was like a lion, and had eagle's wings; and I beheld till the wings were plucked, and it was made to stand upon the feet as a man, and a man's heart was given to it. (7:4.) That these symbols represent the empire of Babylon all interpreters of prophecy agree.

This is, indeed, positively fixed by the prophet, who, addressing Nebuchadnezzar as king of Babylon, says, "Thou art this head of gold." The head of gold, the likeness to a lion, the king of beasts, with wings of an eagle, the king of birds, signify the wealth and glory of this monarchy. The "eagle's wings" denote rapidity of conquest, together with the addition of other governments to the central one, and thus the formation of an extended empire.

"The wings were plucked, and it was lifted up from the earth; or, as Grotius explained, the wings thereof were plucked, wherewith it was lifted up from the earth, denoting cessation of conquests, together with the loss of some already made, as Lydia, Media, and Persia, and general diminution of national territory and strength, until the empire was overthrown by the Medes and Persians.

The pride of Nebuchadnezzar was humbled, and the people became, after their conquests were over, rather after the fall of the empire, more humane; which may be signified according to Newton, by the phrase "a man's heart was given unto it." (Verse 4.)

II. THE MEDEO-PERSIAN EMPIRE.

This is described as "the breast and arms of silver" in the great image, (2:32) a bear, and succession of beasts as being present as it raised itself up on one side, and it had three ribs in the mouth of it, between the teeth of it, and they said unto it, Arise and devour much flesh." (7:5.)

The silver in the image denotes that this empire was

"inferior," as the prophet state') to the "head of gold." The "breast and arals" signify the union of the Medes and Persians in one empire. Ancient historians stigmatize the Medes as being the greatest robbers and spoilers that ever oppressed the nations, which may serve to explain the fact of their being compared to *a bear.*

"Raised itself on one side," may point to its elevation to supreme power by Cyrus, as representing the Persians. "Three ribs in the mouth of it," may point out the kingdoms of Babylon, Lydia, and Egypt, which were oppressed by it. Its cruelty and extent of conquests are signified by its "devouring much flesh."

III. THE GRECIAN OR MACEDONIAN EMPIRE.

This empire supplanted and succeeded the Medeo-Persian, as that had overthrown and succeeded the Babylonian, and is necessarily the as "the belly and thighs represented in the image of brass," (2:32) and in Daniel's vision as a "beast like a leopard, and it had four wings of a fowl; the beast also had four heads; and dominion was given to it."

The brass of the image may signify greater moral baseness than was found in the preceding empires, and yet greater capacity for conquest.

Jerome is more complimentary to the brazen idea: "For among all metals, brass is more vocal and tinkles louder, and its sound is diffused far and wide, that it portended not only the fame and power of the kingdom, but also the eloquence of the Greek language."

The "leopard," a spotted animal, signifies according to Bochart, the different manners of the nations Alexander commanded — a swift animal, and having also four wings, indicating amazing and unparalleled rapidity of conquest.

The "four heads" denote the four kingdoms into which this third empire was divided. In this division Cassander had Macedon and Greece — Lysander, Thrace and Bithynia— Seleucus, Syria —and Ptolemy, Egypt. Of these, Syria and Egypt became far more powerful than the others, as indicated in the two "thighs" of the image.

All writers on this subject identification of the visions of the image, and the brass, which we have noticed, as being in meaning the same, and as pointing to the Babylonian, Medeo-Persian, and Grecian empires.

IV THE ROMAN EMPIRE.

This is represented in the vision of the image by the "legs of iron, and his feet part of iron and part of clay," which latter mixed character is also given of the *toes* of the feet. (2:33-42.) In the vision of the beasts, this fourth beast, for which no appropriate name could be found, is characterized as being "dreadful and terrible, and strong exceedingly; and it had great iron teeth: and it devoured and brake in pieces, and stamped the residue with the feet of it: and it was diverse from all the beasts that were before it: and it had ten horns. I considered the horns, and there came up among them another little horn, before whom there were three of the first horns plucked up; and, behold, in this horn were eyes like the eyes of a man, and a mouth speaking great things." (7:7,8.)

As to the strength of this kingdom, we have this further explanation given by Daniel to Nebuchadnezzar. "And the fourth kingdom shall be strong as iron: forasmuch as iron breaketh in pieces and subdueth all things: and as iron that breaketh all these, shall it break in pieces and bruise."

Corresponding to this is the interpretation given to Daniel by the angel, in chap. 7: "Then I (Daniel) would know the truth of the fourth beast, which was diverse from all the others, exceeding dreadful, whose teeth were of iron, and his nails of brass; which devoured, brake in pieces, and stamped the residue with his feet." (verse 19.) And he was thus answered by the angel: (verse 23) "The fourth beast shall be the fourth kingdom upon earth, which shall be diverse from all kingdoms, and shall devour the whole earth, and shall tread it down, and break it in pieces."

The chronology of the empire thus described as succeeding the Babylonian, the Medeo-Persian, and the

Macedonian, with the remarkable description of its unequalled and resistless power, as given in these visions, would enable almost any schoolboy in the land to identify it as the terrible Roman empire.

"All ancient writers, both Jewish and Christian," says Bishop Newton, "agree with Jerome in explaining the fourth kingdom to be the Roman. Porphyry, who was a heathen and an enemy to Christ, was the first who had maintained another opinion, which has been maintained since by some of the moderns, is yet not only destitute of authority, but is even contrary to the authority of both Scripture and history."

It is a just observation of Mr. Mede, who was as able and consummate a judge as any, in these matters: "The Roman empire to be the fourth kingdom of Daniel, was believed by the church of Israel, both before and in our Saviour's time, received by the disciples and apostles, and the whole Christian Church for the first three hundred years without any known contradiction." "The other opinion" referred to, is the pretension "as absurd as it is singular," that the kingdoms of Syria and Egypt, which belonged to the third kingdom, and are represented by the thighs of brass, constitute the fourth.

The learned Bishop indignantly and successfully refutes this absurd theory of a mere faction of interpreters of prophecy. For the identification of the Roman empire as the fourth kingdom represented in the two visions under consideration, the reader is referred to almost any author who has written on these subjects since the rise of that empire.

This will also more fully appear from further investigation of these prophecies of the fourth empire.

The two legs of the empire, as descriptive of the Roman empire may signify the division of the empire into the eastern and western, with some reference it may be to the dual consulate in the earlier period of its history, when it was specially "diverse from all other kingdoms" in having a republican form of government.

THE BROKEN EMPIRE

The "ten toes" of the image, and the "ten horns" of the beast, which phrases, as all agree, have the same meaning, are the ten primary kingdoms into which the Roman empire was finally divided.

"These are indeed," says Scott, "reckoned up in several ways by different writers, according to the date assigned by the enumeration; but, in general it is clear that the principal kingdoms in Europe at this day sprung from them, and comprise them, excepting some of the more northern regions, and those possessed by the Turks. "

The historian Machiavelli, Mr. Mede, Bishop Lloyd, and Sir Isaac Newton, are quoted by Bishop Newton, as calculating the divisions of the Roman empire for different periods, with the same results as to the number, ten. The Bishop said further. "As if that number had not been fatal in the Roman dominions, it hath been taken notice of on particular occasions; as about A. D. 1240, Eberard, Bishop of Saltsburg, in the diet of Ratisbon. At the time of the Reformation there were also ten; so that the Roman empire was divided into ten in a manner first and last. Mr. Whiston wrote in 1706, 'that as the number of the kingdoms into which the Roman empire in Europe agreeably to the ancient prophecies, was originally divided A. D. 456, was exactly ten, so it is very nearly returned to the same condition.'"

As the third kingdom was divided into four parts, so the fourth was divided into ten. And, as Sir Isaac Newton says, "whatever was their number afterwards, they are still called the ten kings from their first number." Machiavelli's reckoning of the ten toes and the ten horns or kingdoms, is thus: First, the Ostrogoths of Moesia; second, the Visigoths, of Pannonia; third, the Sueves and Aluns of Gascoigne and Spain; fourth, the Vandals in Africa; fifth, the Franks in France; sixth, the Burgundians in Burgundy; seventh, the Heruli and Turingi in Italy; eighth, the Saxons and Angles in Britain; ninth, the Huns in Hungary; and the Lombards, at first upon the Danube, afterwards in Italy.

THE LITTLE HORN. — The fathers as Ireneus, St. Cyril, St. Jerome, and others, interpreted this of Antichrist. Among Protestant writers, both the little horn and Antichrist are understood to mean the Papal power.[2] The three kingdoms subdued by the little horn, are understood by Scott to be those of the Heruli, the Ostrogoths, and the Lombards. Dr. Clarke and Sir Isaac Newton understand by them the Exarchate of Ravenna, the kingdoms of the Lombards, and the States of Rome.

The coincidences of the little horn with the papacy are abundant and decisive. He is the little horn from the smallness of his beginning and of his territorial dominion. "He shall be diverse from the rest," as being an ecclesiastical more than a temporal power."

"And in this horn were eyes like the eyes of a man," denoting superintendence, cunning, policy. "He had a mouth speaking great things," full of boasting, promising to absolve from all sins, threatening with destruction kings and kingdoms, and all others who oppose his authority. "His look was more stout than his fellows" — the Pope assuming superiority, not only over his fellow bishops, but over the kingdoms of the world and to speak great words against the "Most High", or as Symmachus has it, " he shall speak as if he were God,"[3] claiming to be infallible,[4] to forgive sins[5], to be higher than the kings of the earth;[6] all which belong only to God." In Gratian's decretals the Pope hath the title of God given to him." "And he shall wear out the saints of the Most High," by wars, massacres, and inquisitions, persecuting and destroying the faithful servants of Jesus, and the true worshippers of God who protest against his innovations, and refuse to comply with the idolatry practiced by the Church of

---

[2] John 4:3 tells us, "but every spirit that does not acknowledge Jesus is not from God. This is the spirit of the antichrist". So it is impossible that the Pope could be antichrist, as all the Popes recognize and proclaim Christ as the Son of God.

[3] John 21:15-17; Matt. 16:19

[4] John 14: 16-17, 26; Matt. 16:19

[5] Matt. 18:18; John 20:21–23

[6] Matt. 16:18.

Rome; as Bishop Newton explains it. "And he shall think to change times and laws," which Dodd interprets, "appointing fasts and feasts, canonizing persons whom he chooses to call saints, granting pardons and indulgences for sins, instituting new modes of worship utterly unknown to the Christian Church, new articles of faith, new rules, and reversing at pleasure the laws both of God and man." All these particulars are descriptive of the Papal and of no other power. "Until a time, times, and the dividing of time." This is usually understood to be three and a half prophetic years, reckoning 30 days for a month, and days for a year would make 1260 years.

The little horn which unites the spiritual with the civil is the State Church of Europe. And the same idea of the union of church and state which it represents as being itself a dual power, and as growing among the horns on the head of the beast, is set forth in the vision of the metallic image by the union of the clay with the iron in the feet and toes. Such is not indeed the interpretation usually given of this figure.

St. Jerome, who lived to see the incursions of the barbarians, but did not live to see the loftiest pretensions and darkest corruptions of popery in the middle ages, understood it to mean the mixture of barbarism with civilization in the empire, and he has been generally followed in this by Scripture interpreters.

But the identity of the two visions requires the interpretation for which we contend. It is true that the vision of Daniel contains some explanatory circumstances which are not found in that of Nebuchadnezzar; but it is also true that the latter vision contains some very important particulars not found in the former.

The two visions confessedly agree as to leading items. The little horn in the one vision is a very material point, without which it would be incomplete as a representation of history. And is it possible that this item can be left out of the other vision, so that the whole idea of the little horn is ignored, together with that which corresponds with it in the history? If this be so, how can the great image be a correct representation, even in general items of the scope of history it is designed to embrace?

It may be true, that as prophecy has generally a double application, the mixture of clay with iron in the feet and toes of the image may receive illustration from the incursion of barbarians, but is it rational that it should mean this mainly, much less exclusively, when the same figure would explain more forcibly the church and state union in accordance with the truth of history, and with the setting forth in the other vision?

We are strongly in favor, therefore, of Dr. Baldwin's theory as contained in Armageddon, pp. 123-5: "The term, they shall mingle themselves with the seed of men, conveys with great clearness the idea of the degradation of a superior class of persons by mingling with the seed of men in natural affairs.

It is very similar to a passage in Genesis, which speaks of the corruption of the sons of God by uniting with the daughters of men. The mingling with seed of men by this superior class also explained by the notion of a spiritual people uniting with a political power.

Indeed, as no two classes of men can be found in the world corresponding to the two in the text except spiritual and carnal people, the union of these two classes in the fourth empire, must represent church and state union in it, and as in the Roman or fourth great empire, such a union did exist, the case is a very clear one, that the mingled clay represented the Church of Christ corrupted by union with the civil power of Rome represented by the iron."

THE RECONSTRUCTED EMPIRE.

The reconstruction of the Roman empire for which Dr. Baldwin contends, is, we think, represented in the fact that the image is a chronological one, that the toes appear after the feet, that the stone is cut out of the mountain after the toes appear, and yet, that the stone strikes the feet of the image.

This reorganization is a vast and powerful embodiment of the *spirit* of the Roman empire, nay, of all these empires, without special reference to locality or form of government. This reconstruction in spirit is signified in the fact that when the stone strikes the image it finds and destroys the gold and silver, and brass, as well as the iron and clay; indeed, the material of the whole image, both as to successive and specific characteristics, and the spirit that pervades the whole — the spirit of monarchy and despotism.

This is still more clearly set forth in the fact, that when in the other vision it is said that the "beasts had their dominion taken away, their lives were prolonged, or rather a prolonging of life was given them, for a season and time."

This is no representation of the bodies of the beasts, i.e., the nations which exist now where the beasts held their sway, but of the spirit of despotism which, while manifesting specific characteristics in each successive power, passed down the line of dominion until, in the reconstructed feet of the great image, or Rome reorganized in "the last end of the indignation," it is crushed by the "stone cut out of the mountain."

CHAPTER II

FIFTH KINGDOM—THE UNITED STATES OF AMERICA.

The closing symbols in the visions agree—The mountain with the Ancient of days—The stone with the one like the Son of man—The text—Bishop Newton—Civil governments—Tenor of the visions—Necessities of the case—The Ancient of days not God in person, in nature, in revelation, in providence, but in government--Stone not the Church—Date—Baldwin—Conflict with despotism; from without; sudden—Takes the place of the despotism it destroys —Called a "kingdom"—Dr. Clarke's exposition—Dr. Baldwin's—Harmony of the visions   23

IN Nebuchadnezzar's vision, after the entire image representing the four successive monarchies is seen, even down to the feet and toes, two other objects appear—" the mountain," and the "stone cut out of the mountain." In Daniel's vision, the four beasts, which also represent the four monarchies, are succeeded by "the Ancient of days," and "one like the Son of man with the clouds of heaven."

Now, whatever these objects may represent, they assuredly synchronize in the two visions. The "mountain" in the one, is "the Ancient of days" in the other; and the "stone cut out of the mountain" in the former, is the "one like the Son of man" in the latter. The consistency of the visions with each other, as jointly furnishing, as they confessedly do, a dual representation of the same successive kingdoms, requires this interpretation. There are six symbolic representations in each, and these six respectively agree in the two visions. This, as all agree, is the case with four of the symbols, beginning with the first in each vision, and the same is as certainly true of the remaining two.

This is further apparent, from the fact that the same preeminent and perpetual dominion which is ascribed to the "stone cut out of the mountain, is ascribed to the "one like the Son of man." Of the former it is said "it became a great mountain, and filled the whole earth;" and again, that "it shall never be destroyed; and the kingdom shall not be left to other people, but it shall break in pieces, and consume all these kingdoms, and it shall stand for ever." Of the latter it is said, "There was given him dominion, and glory, and a kingdom, that all people, nations, and languages, should serve him: his dominion is an everlasting dominion, which shall not pass away, and his kingdom, that which shall not be destroyed."

And again, "The kingdom and dominion, and the greatness of the kingdom under the whole heaven, shall be given to the people of the saints of the Most High, whose kingdom is an everlasting kingdom, and all dominions shall serve and obey him."

Now this identity of the indivisible characteristics of universal and everlasting dominion (which we shall endeavor to explain in due time) positively fixes the identity of the stone kingdom with the "one like the Son of man." And this again as decisively identifies the mountain with the Ancient of days.

The mountain immediately precedes the stone, just as the Ancient immediately precedes the one like the Son of man. The mountain succeeds the metallic image, even the ten toes of that image, just as "the Ancient" succeeds the four beasts, even the ten horns of the fourth beast.

In the one vision, the mountain intervenes between the image and the stone that breaks it, while in the other "the Ancient" intervenes in the same manner between the four beasts and the "one like the Son of man." On the one hand, the four sections of the image and the four beasts have been found to synchronize; on the other hand, the stone kingdom and the one like the Son of man are the same.

Therefore, the mountain, which intervenes between the four sections of the image and the stone, and the Ancient of days, which intervenes between the four beasts and the "one like the Son of man," must inevitably be the same. Thus Bishop Newton on Prophecy, p. 224: "The *stone* that was cut out of the *mountain* without hands, and became itself a mountain, and filled the whole earth, is explained to be a kingdom, which shall prevail over all other kingdoms, and become universal and everlasting. In like manner, *one like the Son of man* came to the *Ancient of days*, and was advanced to a kingdom which shall prevail likewise over all other kingdoms, and become universal and everlasting." The italicizing in this passage is intended to exhibit more clearly that which the learned prelate designed to show: the "concord and agreement" between these prophecies of Daniel. This "concord and agreement" will more fully appear as we proceed.

The mountain thus identified with the Ancient of days, and the stone cut out of the mountain thus found to synchronize with the one like the Son of man, are civil governments.

The consistency of the visions with themselves and with each other demands this interpretation. The other symbols of the visions confessedly mean civil governments. These latter appear on the same field of vision. They are seen thus to speak with the same prophetic eyes. "The mountain" and "the stone" are as visible and material as the four sections of the metallic image; and if the latter represent civil or outward governments, so do the former.

The Ancient of days, and the one like the Son of man, are just as tangible and visible as the wild beasts that precede them. A man, whether old or young, while differing in character from a beast, is yet no less visible and tangible, and equally suitable as a symbol of outward or civil government.

Indeed, all the symbols being of precisely the same character as to the visible or invisible, and occurring in concatenation in the same visions, they must certainly be understood in the same sense as to this question. If the "mountain" and "stone" — if the "Ancient" and the "one like the Son of man," mean the inward and spiritual, then must the four sections of the image and the four beasts, which are no more material as emblems, also express the inward and spiritual: with this single difference, however, that while the former indicate the spiritual in a good sense, and thus symbolize true religion, the latter indicate the spiritual in a bad sense, and thus symbolize false religion.

In this consistent mode of interpretation, on the ground assumed by the opponent, the civil is utterly lost in the spiritual throughout the visions, and there is no representation of the successive empires of the world. This is manifestly absurd.

But, on the other hand, if the sections of the image and the corresponding beasts symbolize civil governments, then must "the mountain" and "stone," the "Ancient of days" and the "one like the Son of man," which are equally visible and tangible, and which immediately succeed them, also represent civil governments, with, however, this simple difference: that, while the former symbols point to oppressive and corrupt governments, the latter symbols are expressive of free and pure governments.

The interpretation for which we contend arises out of the necessities of the case. If these are not civil governments, what are they?

Is it contended that the "Ancient of days" is the eternal Father? This is Dr. Clarke's view. And yet he says that Almighty God is nowhere else represented as an old man. This fact of itself furnishes strong presumption that he is not so represented here.

Can the position of the great commentator be sustained in view of the prohibition of the immutable law of God, that any visible representation should be made of himself? This is the more impressively true if a hypothesis can be found which will satisfy the name and description here given, without forcing upon the mind the painful alternative of regarding them as unmeaning on the one hand, or as descriptive of the eternal God as an old man on the other.

The Ancient of days on his chariot-throne cannot possibly be a representation of God personally for the above reasons, and for the further one that he is a Spirit, without body or parts. The ascription of eyes to God, which denote his superintendence — of an arm to him, which points out his power, exercised in protection or in wrath, etc., is, to our conception, very different from describing him *personally* as an old man. Accordingly, if this be a description of Almighty

God, it symbolizes him in some particular position, as to human affairs, or as assuming some special *relation* to mankind. Let us investigate this thought.

It will not be contended that the Ancient of days is God in *nature*, appearing at a late period in the world he has made. Nor does he symbolize God in *Revelation*, manifesting himself thus so long after the sacred canon becomes complete. Nor can the Ancient represent the Father in *general providence*.

This providence extends over all nations and through all time. He rules among the inhabitants of the earth. The nations are before him nothing, less than nothing, and vanity. He cutteth off the spirit of princes. He setteth up one and putteth down another. Daniel says to King Nebuchadnezzar, when explaining his dream, "The God of heaven hath given thee a kingdom, power, and strength, and glory." There is a providence at the beginning, as well as at the close of these visions.

If, therefore, the Ancient of days be a manifestation of Almighty God, it is in the form of *government*. This is indicated by the terms "thrones," "sits," "judgment," spoken of in direct reference to the Ancient of days. This cannot be the *Divine government proper*, for that extends over the whole universe, and sweeps through time and eternity.

If there be a Divine government here, it must be embodied in Church or State. We have already noticed the absurdity of supposing that four of the governments in this vision are civil, while the remaining are ecclesiastical. Let us press this subject a little further in this connection.

The Ancient of days cannot be the Church of God. If so, how can it be true, as many affirm, that the stone cut out of the mountain is the Church? For, as we have shown, the Ancient synchronized with *the mountain*, and not with *the stone*, which is identical with the one like the Son of man. The Ancient and the stone cannot, therefore, both symbolize the Church.

The *dates* of the appearance of the Ancient of days and of the cutting of the stone out of the mountain, utterly forbid the supposition that one or both of them should represent the Church of God. Daniel, in his vision, says, "I beheld, and the same horn (the little horn) made war with the saints, and prevailed against them; *until* the Ancient of days came, and judgment was given to the saints of the Most High."

It is said, further, that this political or national "judgment" was not to sit until the little horn had worn out the saints of the Most High, and until they had been given into his hand, "until a time and times and the dividing of time," or, as the commentators reckon, 1260 years.

Thus the Ancient was not to come until the Roman empire, symbolized by the fourth beast, was divided into the ten kingdoms, as answering to the ten horns of the beast, and the papal power signified by the little horn had worn out the saints of the Most High — nearly, according to the common understanding, 1260 years: *nearly*, we say, because the Ancient comes before the destruction of the little horn, and is instrumental in that destruction.

Now the Ancient is identical, as we have seen, with the mountain, out of which the stone is cut. This stone, to which the Church idea is specially attached, cannot, then, be cut out of the mountain before the mountain existed, but necessarily at a period later than that at which the mountain, or Ancient, appears.

Accordingly, Daniel, in describing to the king his vision, says, "This image's head was of fine gold, his breast and his arms of silver, his belly and his thighs of brass, his legs of iron, his feet part of iron and part of clay. Thou sawest *till* that a stone was cut out of the mountain without hands, which smote the image upon his feet that were of iron and clay, and brake them in pieces."

"In the interpretation of the dream, the prophet expressly told the king that *after* he had seen the whole prophetic and chronological image down to the toes, that then he continued to look *forward*, and that in looking *forward* his attention was arrested by the sight of a stone cut out of the mountain without hands.

The expression, 'thou sawest till that a stone was cut out,' indubitably signifies a looking into the future from the toe period, on which his attention had last rested. The term 'thou sawest till' has an expression of futurity in it, absolutely as well as relatively. The word *till*, says Mr. Webster, signifies to the time of, or to the time: as, I will wait *till* next week; occupy *till* I come; saying they would neither eat nor drink till they had killed Paul.

The term 'thou sawest' signified that he continued to look upon events. Now, as all the events in the vision beside the stone occurred chronologically, the expression thou sawest till that a stone was cut out' shows that the looking was chronologically into the future." — *Baldwin*. Let it be noted, too, that it was not a stone that *had been* cut out of the mountain, but the event of the *cutting out* was seen in the vision *after* the feet and toes of the image are seen.

The further explanation of the dream is also decisive upon this point. When the prophet had reached the mixture of iron and clay in the feet and toes, he says, "In the days of *these kings* (or kingdoms) shall the God of heaven set up a kingdom." "Relative words," says Hedge in his Logic, "should be referred to the nearest rather than a remote antecedent." "*These*" kings must be the toe kings of which he had been speaking.

"These" being plural, must refer to the plurality of kingdoms which the prophet had spoken of as existing in the Roman empire, as now marking the period when the stone is cut out of the mountain. To apply the term "these" to all these empires, meaning that somewhere during the successive ages of their history the God of heaven should set up a kingdom is to depart from all perspicuity, and confuse, as to dates, the whole vision.

The phrase "these kings" could not apply to the rise of Christianity, for the Roman Empire then existed as *one* kingdom, to which, of course, a plural term could not be applied. But the rise of the kingdom in question during the broken state of the empire, coincides with the period in the chronology of the vision the prophet occupies when making this exposition, with the fact that the stone was cut out of the mountain after the feet and toes of the image appear, and with the fact that even the Ancient of days did not come until after the ten horns of the beast had arisen, and even the little horn had long worn out the saints of the Most High.

That the stone is not the Church of Christ is also plain from its *work,* and from the *manner* in which that work is performed. The first business of the stone after being cut out of the mountain, is to break in pieces the feet of the image, or the reconstructed Roman empire. It is first seen in violent and deadly conflict with civil despotism, whereas the Church, as such, has nothing to do with the State. In the prophecies of the Bible she is represented as being corrupted by such connection wherever it occurs.

The stone comes in conflict with despotism *from without,* whereas the action of the Church upon an empire or nationality is from within. Christian truth, as leaven, diffuses itself silently, imperceptibly, till the whole is leavened. It may in this way enlighten, refine, and elevate a people, and by preparing them for higher forms of government, may indirectly bring about the adoption of such forms. But the violent, destructive action from without, as of the stone upon the feet of the image, cannot possibly be realized in any legitimate movement of the Church of God.

The action of the stone upon the feet of the image is *sudden* and *complete.* The idea expressed is affirmed by Dr. Clarke to be that of the hurling of a stone from a Roman catapult. The effect is the immediate and utter destruction of the image. The influence of the Church is not only silent and unseen, but *gradually progressive,* and cannot possibly be illustrated by the conflict of the stone with the image.

The stone *takes the place* of the image after its destruction, and finally becomes "a great mountain, and fills the whole earth." The fact that the stone not only destroys the image, but supplants it in the inheritance of the greatness and glory and dominion, is conclusive as to its being a civil government, though different in character from the image.

The stone is expressly called a *"kingdom,"* just as the sections of the image and the beasts are kingdoms. And this kingdom is identified with "the *people of the saints"—not* the saints personally or collectively, but the people of the saints, or a glorious Christian nationality, possessing the greatness and glory under the whole heaven.

The fact that the date of the appearance of the stone kingdom is positively fixed as being after the feet and toes of the image appear, or in the broken state of the Roman empire, together with the other considerations we have named, are conclusive of the civil character of the stone kingdom.

What sad work the *usual exposition,* which identifies the stone with the Church, makes of the imagery and chronology of these visions! Take that of Dr. Clarke as a specimen. Whereas the prophet plainly tells the king that from the toe period of the great chronological image he saw "till that a stone was cut out of the mountain," the commentator makes him see *backward* from that period, to the rise of the Christian Church in Judea, many centuries before. And he understands, further, that the mountain is the Roman empire, which is characterized in the vision itself as the legs of iron, and the feet part of iron and part of clay.

How the Church was cut out of the Roman empire cannot, we think, be satisfactorily explained. Such expositions illustrate the fact that the vision of prophecy was shut up until the time of the end. Bishop Newton says of these very predictions, "It is the nature of such prophecies not to be perfectly understood till they are fulfilled. The best comment upon them will be their fulfillment."

Our conclusion is, that neither the Ancient of days, nor the stone cut out of the mountain, symbolizes the Church of Christ.

If, then, the Ancient of days be understood to be Almighty God, (and there *is* a Divine idea in the symbol,) he is not a revelation of him *personally,* nor in *creation,* nor his *word,* nor in general *providence,* but in *a nationality,* raised up by him as an instrument for the accomplishment of great and beneficent changes in the condition of mankind. And as he certainly did in ancient times raise up a nationality for such *a* purpose, it is surely not unreasonable that he should in the latter ages select one for the accomplishment of still greater good for the human race.

Our business in this part of the investigation is with the fifth kingdom; but in order to prove this to be outward and visible, it is necessary to show the same to be true of the sixth, with which it must agree in spirit, and for which it prepares the way. If one of these be visible and outward, so is the other. And we have endeavored to prove both to be of this character.

Here it may be proper to notice Dr. Baldwin's obvious error in explaining these closing symbols of the visions under discussion. He correctly understands the Ancient of days to be the fifth kingdom, or the United States of America, but makes this synchronize, not with the *mountain*, in the other vision, but with the *stone* cut out of the mountain; whereas, as Bishop Newton affirms, and as we have shown from the text, the stone is identical, not with the Ancient, but with the one like the Son of man.

This confounding of the fifth kingdom in the one vision with the sixth in the other, leaves him the awkward task of accounting for the mountain in one vision, and the one like the Son of man in the other, when there is nothing to synchronize with them.

As to the mountain, he *says* it symbolizes a government, either civil or ecclesiastical. And inasmuch as the stone is a Christian nationality, a kingdom set up by the God of heaven, it is cut out of the Church: not cut off from the mountain as a stone cut off from a cliff or a ledge of rocks composing a mountain, but the change of the mountain substance into a double nature, just as we say a statue is cut out of a block of marble, or a vase is cut out of alabaster."

But let it be noted that the figure is not the carving of a statue out of a rock, but the cutting of a rock out of the mountain, without reference to the statue at all. Now the simple cutting of a rock out of the mountain must be very different from (1.) changing the mountain substance into a rock; (2.) carving the rock into an image, which is, unless the mountain substance be already a rock, the precise process we understand to be involved in the exposition under notice.

Further, if the idea were that of chiseling a rock into a statue, it would mean the transformation of the Church, as such, into the State, so that the Church really becomes the State, which is absurd.

In another place our friend Dr. B. makes the mountain out of which the stone is cut to be the throne on which Ancient sits. The Ancient he identifies with the stone, and the Ancient's throne with the mountain. This is precisely confounding the stone with the mountain after it is taken from it, whereas they are as distinct as any two sections of the image, or two beasts, after one has succeeded the other. The mountain and stone are *two;* whereas the Ancient on his throne is *one,* expressed according to the Doctor's own correct theory under dual symbols.

Again: the one like the Son of man is, according to the Doctor, not a government *distinct* from the Ancient, but simply a *change* of form, answering to the stone's becoming *a* great mountain and filling the earth. But the Ancient, and the one like the Son of man, are as distinct from each other as any two of the beasts or sections of the image, or as the mountain and the stone, with which they respectively agree.

But when the mountain is identified with the Ancient of days, and the stone with the one like the Son of man, and the growth of the stone into a mountain filling the earth, with the universal and eternal dominion of the one like the Son of man, we have the latter parts of the visions as beautifully and harmoniously complete as the former. "The concord and agreement" of the two visions are thus fully seen, and they become, indeed, as Mr. Mede says, "The sacred calendar and great almanac of prophecy."

This chapter is designed to pave the way for proofs, both presumptive and direct, that the mountain and the Ancient of days jointly symbolize the United States of America

CHAPTER III
THE UNITED STATES—CONTINUED.

The mountain and the ancient identified with the mountain of the Lord's house, or Israel restored—The typical system—The church—The state—Israel restored not spiritually—not literally—but in the antitype.

HAVING shown that the mountain and the ancient of days are identical, and that they represent a civil government, we shall endeavor to establish their reference to the United States of America.

It may be proper, however, at once, to identify these prophecies of the fifth kingdom with a class of predictions in the other prophets, which, though unconnected with this great chain of empire, refer unmistakably to this same fifth kingdom.

The symbol of this power in the king's dream, is the mountain. "Mountain" signifies, as we have seen, a government — a civil government. It is not *a* mountain indefinitely, but specifically *the* mountain—the great prophetic mountain familiar to the prophets as the central glorious christian nationality of future times. It is "the mountain of the Lord's house, established in the top of the mountains." (Isaiah 2:2.) (Micah. 5:1.) This is further manifested from the corresponding symbol in the prophet's vision.

It appears, as we have seen, late in the Christian era, and yet is characterized as an old man, styled the ancient of days with hair white as wool. These items signify old age. Now, as we have seen, if the ancient symbolize God, it is God, not personally, but God in a government or nationality. And the machinery here employed must describe the nationality to which it applies.

The symbol can be fulfilled only by a nationality that

existed in "ancient" times; and ceasing to be, is now revived — once existing in type, now in antitype. The same is plain from the mountain, as identified with the mountain of the Lord's house. This is no other than Israel restored; the nationality that God raised up as his peculiar government revived, according to numerous and explicit predictions "in the last days."

Isaiah, amid his expostulations with Israel, either literal or restored, or both, utters this prophecy of the mountain of the Lord's house. (Is. 2:2.) This is still more obvious in the connection of the prophecy as repeated in Micah 4:1. In the verse immediately preceding it, is written: "Therefore shall Zion for your sakes be ploughed as a field, and Jerusalem shall become heaps, and the mountain of the house as the high places of the forest."

Let this be applied to the literal Jerusalem, which is connected with the mountain of the house which is to be destroyed. "But," in contrast with this, "in the last days it shall come to pass that the mountain of the house of the Lord shall be established in the top of the mountains." And this mountain or government is again in the next verse spoken of as "Zion" and "Jerusalem."

This identity of the mountain with Israel in the type and in the antitype, is further signified in the fact that Zion is called "the holy mountain."

The same is plain from the fact that in the prophets the same glory which is ascribed to the "mountain" is ascribed to Israel restored in the last days.

The Patriarchal and Jewish dispensations were full of types. A type is defined by Webster as a "a sign, a symbol, a figure of something to come;" by Richard Watson, as "an example, pattern, or general similitude to a person, event, or thing which is to come." Adam was a type or figure of him that was to come. Melchizedek was made like unto God. Abraham was enabled to see Christ's day. Isaac was received from the dead in a figure. The paschal lamb was typical of "our passover slain for us."

The whole Jewish system was a typical system. That

system consisted of two general departments — the civil and ecclesiastical, or the state and the church.

That the ecclesiastical department was of a typical character is admitted on all hands. Their religious ordinances were a figure "for the times then present," "shadows of good things to come." Their tabernacle typified the greater and more perfect tabernacle not made with hands. Their high priest was typical of the High Priest of our profession. Their sacrifices had reference to the one great sacrifice for sins.

Now, if the state was not like the church typical (1) they did not harmonize. They were like the legs of the lame, not equal. (2) The one was full of meaning for all time; the other was restricted and temporary in signification. (3) The one was a glorious success, notwithstanding gloomy and protracted reverses, unless the cause of God should finally fail in the world; the other, mostly local as it was in influence, and temporary in duration, would seem to be a failure. It cannot be true that this sublime system, as the work of Almighty God, should thus fail in either of its great departments.

Accordingly, the prophets assure us that the old Israel was but typical of, and preparatory to, Israel restored in the mountain of the Lord's house, when, too, the church department should shine forth in its final antitypical splendor, as "the law should go forth out of Zion, and the word of the Lord from Jerusalem." These prophecies of Israel's restoration are so literal and circumstantial as to be incapable of a spiritual signification.

Take such as the following, as specimens: "For lo! the days come, saith the Lord, that I will bring again the captivity of my people Israel and Judah saith the Lord; and I will cause them to return to the land that I gave to their fathers and they shall possess it. (Jer. 30:3.) "I will sow the house of Judah and the house of Israel with the seed of man and with the seed of beast. I will bring again the captivity of my people Israel, and they shall build the waste cities and inhabit them." (Amos 9:14.)

When this restoration occurs, the land of Israel is to be the center of immigration for the nations, the religious capital of the world. The Lord is to be "a crown of glory and a diadem of beauty," and his servant David is to reign over his people and the "remnant of Jacob shall be in the midst of many people as a dew from the Lord, as the showers the grass, that tarrieth not for man; as a lion among the beasts of the forest; as a young lion among the flocks of sheep; who, if he go through, both treadeth down, and teareth in pieces, and none can deliver."

Such passages, and they are numerous in the prophets, indicate the restoration of Israel, and the greatness and glory of the tribes thus finally restored. What is the character of this restoration of Israel

As already observed, it will not be spiritual, as realized in the prosperity of the church, as such, in future times.

The bringing back of the people of Israel to their land, the successful pursuit of agriculture there, the erection of a glorious nationality amid civil conflicts, all of which, and much more is foretold, utterly forbid this interpretation.

Nor will it be the literal restoration of the Jews to the land of Judea.

There are three things essential to a type: 1. It must point to something future, answering to itself, which is called the antitype. 2. This anti-type, while in a sense an ideal continuation of the type, is never a literal repetition of itself. Not a solitary type can be found in the Scriptures, which is fulfilled in the antitype by a literal repetition of itself. 3. The antitype, thus answering to the type, and yet differing from it, is far more glorious than the type.

There is certainly no reason for departure from these principles in the case before us, but even peculiar reasons for adhering to them. The term Israel signifies one who prevails with God. And there is the same difference between carnal Israel and spiritual Israel, as there was between ungodly Jacob and prevailing Israel. They are not all Israel who are of Israel.

Abraham too, was the father of the faithful in a much

higher and sublimer sense than of the Jewish people, and was heir of the world as truly as he was of Canaan. The Jews as his natural seed, were typical of Christians as his spiritual seed. Thus "he is not a Jew who is one outwardly," but "he is a Jew who is one inwardly." The promise is thus sure to all the seed.

It is expressly stated that David should be the ruler of Israel restored. This is assuredly David in the antitype, who is the root and the offspring of David, our Lord Jesus Christ.

As the ruler is found in the antitype, so must be the kingdom he rules. This cannot be the literal Jewish nationality rebuilt, but that which answers to it in Christian times, and is far more glorious. Is the final Israel to consist of the literal Jewish people? Why have they maintained their separate existence as a people? Because of their rejection of the Saviour and adherence to the old religion, which forbids their amalgamation with other nations.

And is it credible that such stubborn, persevering rejection of Christ will be rewarded by their almost miraculous conversion, and elevation to the spiritual leadership of the Christian world, while Christians who have suffered for ages for the testimony of Christ, are assigned an inferior and secondary position in the enterprise of converting the world to God?

So far is this from being true, that it is expressly stated that the Jews will not be converted till the *fullness* of the Gentiles shall be brought in. More of this in another place.

In accordance with this general typical character, the land of Judea is typical of a broader and more glorious land of the restored Israel of God. Palestine is very small, has meager agricultural, commercial, and manufacturing advantages; is occupied and surrounded by semi-barbarous people. Can it become the center of emigration for the nations, and in all respects, in temporal, political, and religious prosperity and power, the capital of the world? Not unless the laws of nature and of human society are radically and totally changed.

Why is there a lingering desire among the Jews to return

to Palestine? Because of their persistent adherence to the old religion, which required the worship of God at Jerusalem. Their conversion to Christianity would enable them to appreciate the words addressed by our Saviour to the woman of Samaria: "The hour cometh, when ye shall neither in this mountain, nor yet at Jerusalem, worship the Father. God is a spirit: and they that worship him must worship him in spirit and in truth."

The prophetic periods cannot be far at any rate, according to most writers on prophecy, from their termination when the mystery shall be finished. And yet there are no indications of the restoration of the Jewish people to their own land, as a means of finishing this mystery.

This whole idea of making the typical nationality of old Israel simply repeat itself in the anti-type, is destructive of the relationship between the Jewish system as the type, and the Christian system as the antitype. If one type is to be fulfilled by a literal repetition of itself, why is it not so of all other types? Thus, the theory carried to its utmost extent, would thoroughly Judaize Christianity itself.

For these, and many other reasons that might be named, we regard the literal theory as entirely impossible and absurd.

We conclude that the nationality of ancient Israel is to be restored in a great Christian nationality, sustaining the same relations to God and the world; answering to and yet differing from and more glorious than the old type; in keeping with the relations which always subsist between the type and the antitype.

Is it still insisted that the specific promises that the Jews shall return to their own land, the land wherein their fathers' dwelt must be understood literally? We answer, that the same identity is expressed elsewhere between the type and the antitype.

Thus it is said that David shall rule Israel restored, and as plainly asserted elsewhere that Christ, his antitype, shall do the same. Christ *is* our passover, and yet not the veritable lamb slain in the passover.

Now in this case the type cannot be spiritually fulfilled in the antitype, for Christ was as really slain as was the lamb, his type. The identity in meaning is expressed, and yet the antitype was different from and far more glorious than the type. Thus the language in question cannot be spiritualized, for there is a real land of Israel restored. But this land of restoration is the antitype, and while this is identified, as in other cases, with the type, it is also different from and far more glorious than the type.

Now, if admitting that the Jews will finally settle in Judea, this will be but one of the *results* of the restoration of Israel in the antitype, or the establishment of the mountain of the Lord's house in the top of the mountains, and does not affect the argument at all, as we shall see more clearly as we proceed.

We have identified the mountain, in the king's vision, with the Ancient of days, in the prophet's vision; also the mountain, with the mountain of the Lord's house and Israel restored.

Again, we have found the mountain of the Lord's house to agree with the mountain in the vision, and Israel restored to synchronize with the Ancient of days. These four are thus seen to be identical. And our next task is to bring proofs from this fourfold source, to show that the United States constituted the first embodiment of the restored Israel of God.

CHAPTER IV
THE UNITED STATES — CONTINUED.

The Fifth Kingdom the United States—Proofs presumptive and direct—United States probably in prophecy —Her extent, growth, power, a Free Nationality—Date of the Fifth Power—Judges— The Little Horn —Outside the Roman Empire.

THE mountain, or the mountain of the house of the Lord, the Ancient of days, or Israel restored, unitedly symbolize the United States of America.

Our proofs of this proposition are both presumptive and direct.

A few presumptive proofs may be given.

If the United States are not represented by the mountain and the Ancient of days, as corroborated and explained by coincident prophecies, then are they excluded from the great system of prophecy. They cannot of course be symbolized by any section of the image down to its toes, or by the successive beasts even to the horns of the fourth. No one will imagine this to be the case. There is then no place for the glorious nationality of the New World up to this very point in the vision. That it is not represented later will hereafter appear. If the model republic as it has existed is not represented here, it is excluded from the scope of distinctive prophetic vision.

Is it at all probable that the great republic should be left out of prophecy?

Consider her territorial extent as being ten times larger than France and England combined, one sixth less only than the fifty-nine or sixty empires, states, and republics of Europe, and of equal or larger extent than any of the old empires that preceded her in history — her rapid amazing growth in population and all the elements of national greatness, her position as the representative of the entire New World — her sublime system of government, the wonder and admiration of the world — the mighty and universal influence she has wielded — the fact that no nation has been found to cope with her in war or on the field of general politics, manifesting the further fact that she has actually held the reins of preeminent dominion — and in view of these and other facts and considerations that might be adduced, is it at all probable that the great western power should be left out of prophecy?

The question derives still greater force from the character of the United States as a free republican government. That the Almighty is opposed to despotism is plain from the express declarations of his word — from the fact that despotic governments are characterized as wild beasts which he will providentially destroy — from his selection of ancient Israel, a free republic, as his peculiar people and from his decision that their request of a king was the rejection of himself.

We can call the Most High to account for none of his matters; but can we suppose from data thus furnished in his word that he would bring prominently forward on the arena of prophetic vision the despotisms he hates and will destroy, and utterly ignore such a great and free nationality as the United States, which accorded in spirit with the teachings of his word and exercised an influence so vast and beneficial upon the affairs of mankind?

Let it be asked again with emphasis, Has distinctive prophetic vision totally failed to discover the New World? Does it cease with the toes of the image, the horns of the fourth beast, the fragments of the old Roman empire? Is there to be no national center for the succeeding scene of glory, as there has been for the preceding season of gloom and sorrow? If the United States be not the fifth kingdom, it is because the fifth symbols, and, by consequence, the sixth also, are wholly spiritual in their character. This, as we have seen, cannot be the case.

Let us notice the direct proofs that the mountain and the Ancient of days symbolize the United States of America. The date at which the mountain of the Lord's house should appear, is given in the collateral prophecies referred to as "the last days." This phrase would be naturally understood to mean the Christian era, characterized by the apostle even in his day as "the last times." It must further signify a late period in the Christian era; for, as we have seen, this is none other than Israel restored, which event is located by the prophets, as all agree, many ages after the appearance of Christianity in the world.

The vision of the Ancient of days fixes the date more specifically. Not to insist at all on Dr. Baldwin's calculations, which come down with remarkable precision to July 4, 1776, as the *first* period, it is clear from Daniel's vision, that the fifth kingdom was to appear after the ten kingdoms symbolized by the ten toes of the image and the ten horns of the fourth beast had arisen. It was to appear further after the little horn arose; after that power had long worn out the saints of the Most High and shortly before the overthrow of his temporal dominion.

In connection with the appearance of the Ancient, the prophet says, "I beheld then because of the great words which the horn spake, I beheld even till the beast was slain, and his body destroyed, and given to the burning flame." Dan. 7:11. The beast in this verse is the little horn itself, and not the Roman empire out of which it sprung. His body or temporal dominion is consumed. And this consuming is placed after the Ancient of days came, and in immediate connection, verse 13, with the coming of one like the Son of man. In further explanation, verses 21, 22, the prophet says this little horn "made war with the saints and prevailed against them, until the Ancient of days came, and judgment was given to the saints of the Most High." And again: The saints, were to be given into the hand of the little horn "until, a time and times and the dividing of time." This period is according to the learned generally, 1260 years.

This number is reached by understanding the time and times and dividing of time, to be three and a half times, or years; which, reckoning as the Jews did, thirty days to the month, would amount to 1260 prophetic days, or years. This period commenced, as the majority of interpreters think, with the decree of Phocas constituting the Pope supreme head of the Church, in 606.[7] These calculations, and we shall not here

---

[7] Peter was appointed directly by our Divine Lord to be head of His Church. Matt. 16:18. Emperor Phocas, of the Eastern Roman Empire, in 606 by his decree merely recognized what all Christendom knew, i.e. that the Pope, as successor of St. Peter, was the Universal Bishop - as opposed to the pretentions of the Bishop of Constantinople.

examine the question of their correctness, would place the destruction of the body of the little horn within the decade upon which we have now entered.

As a matter of fact, the States of the Church have, within a few months, been absorbed by the kingdom of Italy, and the body of the little horn is in effect no more, unless it should revive for a little season amid the convulsions soon to occur in Europe. The Ancient was to arise as a great and glorious power before, and not very long before, the current period, and can be no other than the United States.

This conclusion is abundantly confirmed by the fact, that the Ancient was to be instrumental in the destruction of the little horn just as truly, though apparently not so directly, as the stone was to break in pieces the reconstructed. Roman empire. The horn made war with the saints "until the Ancient of days came." It seems that from the Ancient, judgment proceeded against the horn, which was to be executed by others.

Now the doctrine or fiery stream of American freedom, civil and ecclesiastical, has scorched and withered papal no less than other despotisms. And the more so as it was in this case a compound influence against a compound despotism. It is entirely manifest that the rapid decline and final extinction of popery, as a temporal power, are directly traceable to the popular revolutions of Europe beginning with the French revolution, including the policy and wars of Napoleon, which shook that power to its center, together with succeeding convulsions, embracing those of 1859-60. And these popular revolutions are in their turn as directly traceable to the example, the doctrine, and the influence of the United States. The Ancient of days must be therefore the United States, because here and here only is this coincidence to be found.

The fifth kingdom was to arise outside the Roman empire alike in its united and its broken state. The Ancient of days is entirely distinct from the fourth beast and his horns. And the fact that he appears during the existence of these horns and of the little horn, is further indicative of the fact that in locality or territory he is separate and distinct from them. Dr. Baldwin calculates that the ten thousand times ten thousand who *stood before* the Ancient, amount to about the actual population of Europe at the rise of the United States, while the thousand thousands, i.e., three thousand, would, by the same rule of multiplication, amount to the three million then inhabiting the United States.

The fact that the fifth kingdom is outside the Roman empire is still more manifest from the king's vision. The stone strikes the feet of the image, or reconstructed empire, from without. It is outside therefore the Roman empire, even in its reconstruction. Now, the stone is cut out of the mountain, and the territorial locality is of course the same. If therefore the stone was outside the Roman empire, so was the mountain, or fifth kingdom, out of which it is taken.

Now, the Roman empire included western Asia, northern Africa, and Europe as far west as the British Isles.

There has been no great and glorious Christian nationality arising outside the Roman empire, and arising too, as we have seen, after it was broken into fragments, and after the little horn or popery had long existed, and instrumental in the destruction of the little horn, excepting the United States of America. The great republic must therefore, of necessity, be symbolized as the fifth kingdom, by the mountain, or mountain of the house of the Lord, and by the Ancient of days, or Israel restored in the antitype. We can see, even at this stage of the investigation, no escape from this conclusion.

It seems to be intimated that the fifth kingdom should be of comparatively short duration.

In the king's dream, the Roman empire is represented as the legs, feet, and toes of the image, while the mountain is mentioned as intervening between the toes and the stone. The empire, according to the symbols and to history, occupies a vast tract in the annals of mankind. The apparently casual mention of the mountain, may signify its short duration as compared with that of the preceding empire, as well of that everlasting kingdom which succeeds.

The same seems indicated in the other vision. The ancient does not appear "until" the little horn had worn out the saints for a long period; and when he had succeeded in destroying the little horn, he gives way after a brief and glorious day to the one like the Son of man.

When the other prophets speak of Israel restored, they almost immediately speak, as we shall see, of Israel in trouble and Israel divided. After the mention of the mountain of the house of the Lord, as in Micah, the scene is soon presented of the travail of the daughter of Zion, and the birth of a man child, or final nationality. From all our prophetic sources we gather intimations that the fifth kingdom is of brief duration. The United States existed as a glorious republic eighty-four years.

The fifth kingdom is of vast extent of territory.

Now, the mountain is not mentioned in the original statement of the dream, excepting that the inference is furnished that as the stone kingdom is cut out, there must be an antecedent something from which it is taken, and that as the stone is a nationality, this antecedent, of whose nature it must partake, is also a nationality or civil government. This original statement is very brief, and this hiatus is filled, in the explanation following, by "the mountain." This apparently casual mention has served to divert attention from the importance of the mountain, and illustrates the fact that the vision of prophecy was closed and sealed up until the time of the end.

But if the mountain is left out of the original account of the dream, the same is true of the toes, which are mentioned afterward. And if this does not underrate the importance of the toes, neither does it deny the value of the mountain. While the latter is not so conspicuous as the stone, yet as it here appears, and especially as synchronizing with the Ancient and with the mountain of the house of the Lord, it has great value of its own.

The term mountain, as here used, signifies not only government, but as compared with the preceding symbols, and with the facts stated as to the stone that it became "a *great mountain,*" and filled the whole earth, it signifies a government of large territorial extent.

The same is inferable from its position in this and the other vision. In both it so intervenes between the preceding empires and the final kingdom as to transfer the reins of empire from the former to the latter. And as the preceding empires were immense, and as the final one becomes so, such must be the case with the one that fills the intervening vacuum. In the collateral prophecies, too, this fifth empire is represented as the center of the world's emigration, which can he true only of a large country.

The same is more clearly seen in the fact that the mountain is of sufficient territorial vastness to give off from itself, and out of itself, the final controlling government of the world. The stone itself is of sufficient size and strength (though not wholly its own) to break in pieces the great image. This stone is not, it would seem, cut off as a distant appendage, but "cut out" of the main body of the government; and while carrying with it the main strength of the government, leaves the most of its territory behind. For when the stone is cut out, it is plain that the largest part of the mountain still remains. Before this cutting out, the stone certainly constituted part of the mountain, the two forming one nationality, and it necessarily follows that it was one of immense extent.

This territorial vastness is further manifest, from the fact that the Ancient of days has his throne on wheels. Pillars would denote fixedness, but wheels signify motion. Is not this expressive of a moving, advancing, expanding nationality — one too, that has for its rapid development a vast region to be overrun gradually, and yet rapidly, by these chariot wheels. And this advance on wheels signifies that the large country thus brought under sway, is not a distant province across the sea, but a vast united territory, such as the great republic has alone possessed.

The fifth kingdom is a vast western wilderness settled by emigration, and rapidly developed into a great Christian nationality.

A Wilderness — "In the latter years thou shalt come into the land that is brought back from the sword, and is gathered out of many people, against the mountains of Israel, which have been *always waste;* but is brought forth out of many nations, and they shall dwell safely all of them." (Ezek. 38:8.)

Here it is expressly stated that the land of Israel restored has been always waste. It is also a land brought back from the sword. The sword symbolizes war. Is it not here stated that the land of Israel restored was a wilderness — had never been cultivated — and yet was inhabited? inhabited, too, by people whose employment was not agriculture but war? This savage people must have been divided into nations or tribes, as signified by the fact that their business was war.

The same land is stated to have been a wilderness "from of old." The prophet further refers to all the "inhabited parts of the country," plainly intimating that after the settlement of Israel, there were parts of the country not inhabited. How well this agrees with the idea of national expansion set forth in the moving wheels of the Ancient's chariot throne. All this is true of the country occupied and developed by the United States, as seen in the rapid addition of territories and states to her dominion.

A Western Land. — "Surely the isles shall wait for me, and the ships of Tarshish first, to bring thy sons from far." (Isa. 60:9.)

"The term 'isles' was applied anciently to Europe and all countries west of Asia Minor.

Those vast countries supposed to exist in the Atlantic, west of Gibraltar, are also termed isles, by both Plato and Diodorus Siculus." — Baldwin. The waiting of the isles, is precisely applicable to the mountains of Israel, that were always waste until settled and cultivated by the modern Israel of God.

Tarshish was the most ancient name of Spain, by whose ships the waiting isles were "first" discovered.

"To bring thy sons from far," signifies the immense distance of these isles from the countries from which emigration should come to them.

The emigrants being carried in ships to the isles, signifies that they lie across the ocean. Indeed, the term isles would imply the necessity of a voyage to reach them.

But they shall fly upon the shoulders of the Philistines toward the west. (Isa. 11:14.)

Flying upon the shoulders of others, means transportation by others. Toward the west, signifies that that is the direction of the Israel of God. It is emigration to the far off isles across the sea, or the western land that was "always waste."

The place of Israel restored being the western world, agrees with the fact that the stone, and by consequence the mountain out of which it is taken, is outside the Roman empire; and with the fact that while the Ancient of days was surrounded by thousand thousands, the ten thousand times ten thousand stood *before* him for judgment in the region beyond his own domain, and occupied by the little horn and kindred despotisms.

The land of Israel restored is the great center of emigration for the nations of the world. In the prophecies of the mountain of the house of the Lord, it said that "all nations shall flow unto it." (Isa. 11:2.) This fact repeatedly spoken of by the prophets, is intimated in the fact that the fifth kingdom, though of short duration, is nevertheless a vast mountain, and that the Ancient moves forward on the wheels of his chariot throne.

The vast emigration in which Israel is gathered out of many nations, answers to and fulfils the Scriptures, which predict that God's peculiar people shall be brought back from their dispersions. One prophet says, "I will surely assemble thee, Jacob, all of thee." (Mic. 2:12.) Another conveys the assurance that the outcasts of Israel, and the dispersed of Judah from the four corners of the earth, shall be assembled. (Isa. 11:12.) Another says, "I will gather the remnant of my flock out of all countries whither I have driven them." (Jer. 23:13.) "I will bring again the captivity of my people Israel and Judah."

And will the ten lost tribes of "Israel" as well as "Judah," be brought back to literal Palestine, and will that be the center of emigration for all nations, and the capital of the world? Is it not impossible and absurd? Israel fallen in the valley of dry bones, even very dry, were to be raised to life. The identity of the resurrection bodies is seen in sameness of bones, the difference in newness of flesh and sinews, and skin and spirit; and the antitype is rendered still further glorious by the multiplication of the bones into an exceeding great army.

The wilderness state of the land of Israel previous to its settlement, answers to the desolations of many generations which have overtaken literal Judea.

The little country of Judea was typical of a broader and more glorious land, so vast as that the great mountain occupies only the inhabited parts of the country, and the Ancient of days sits to the very last upon his chariot throne, whose flying wheels are as burning fire.

The old type was in the old world, the glorious antitype is in the new, as the final theatre of God's kingdom before the renovation of the earth by fire.

The land is the antitype of Judea, the people, as Christians, the antitype of the Jews; and the glorious, pure, energetic nationality symbolized by the Ancient of days, fulfils the nationality of God's ancient people. In no particular is there, or could there be, a repetition of the type, but everywhere the glorious antitype appears. And this antitype appears, as to its first realization, in the United States, and cannot possibly be found, according to prophetic intimations as to time, locality, and description, anywhere else.

The fifth kingdom, or Israel restored, is a free government. Such was ancient Israel, and such must be the restored Israel of God.

The image and the beasts confessedly symbolize despotic governments — such is the meaning of the symbols and such is the witness of history on the subject. The stone is in entire contrast with the image which it breaks in pieces, and this contrast necessarily implies free government. The mountain was of necessity of the same general character with the stone before the stone was cut out of it, though a change in character might have occasioned the separation of the stone. The mountain is then a free government.

The same is indicated in the other vision by the contrast between the one like the Son of man and the glorious Ancient of days, with whom he obviously agrees in spirit, and the wild beasts that preceded them.

The utter contrast of these symbols with those of preceding despotisms, is indicative of the highest ideal of free government, both in spirit and in form. This highest ideal in spirit would allow the utmost freedom of the individual man, consistent with the peace and safety of the body politic.

The contrast in this respect is indicated in the difference in spirit of humane men, one of whom is even like the meek and lowly "Son of man," and the terrible beasts of prey, and is seen further in form between the erect form of man, with benignity and intelligence in his face, and that of the prone, and filthy, and voracious brute.

The same, both as to spirit and form, is seen in the stone, which, as the opposite of despotism, is certainly the final ideal of free government. This being a free republic, such, also, must be the character of the mountain, out of which it is taken, and with which it agrees,

Ancient Israel was a theocratic democracy, and the promise as to Israel restored is, that "I will restore thy judges as at the first, and thy counselors as at the beginning." Again: "Their nobles shall be of themselves, and their governor from the midst of them."

The fifth kingdom or Israel restored, is a federative republic.

The preceding despotisms all included many departments, provinces, or kingdoms in one; and it would be reasonable to expect that a nationality, so vast and so mighty as to succeed them in preeminent dominion, should be, in this respect, similar. The case is stronger, in view of the fact that the fifth government is a free republic A kingdom, however great in extent, may be ruled by the sword as one. But a vast free government, resting on the consent of the governed, could hardly avoid oppression somewhere, unless its action were modified and restrained by local governments.

That such is the character of the fifth kingdom, the Scriptures clearly teach. The cutting of the stone out of the mountain implies a blocking off of some of those separate subordinate governments in a confederate republic, rather than the tearing out of an integral portion of a vast consolidated empire. And it would require less of effort and violence to do the former than the latter.

Now, this mountain in the king's vision is no other than the mountain of the Lord's house, spoken of by Isaiah 2:2, and Micah 5:1. Note the description: "The house of the Lord" is his church. "The mountain" which, in the prophetic symbols, signifies government, is the nationality connected with the house of God—a glorious christian government. This is established in the top of other "mountains," also symbolic of governments.

Here is a government established in the top of other governments — the federal government in the top of the state governments. This is in accordance with the interpretation of mountains, as laid down in Horne's Introduction, Vol. II. p. 466: "High mountains, and lofty hills, denote kingdoms, republics, states and cities." The reader is referred to dictionaries of symbols on this subject.

We cannot surely explain this passage literally; and to understand "the mountain" in a symbolic sense, signifying a government, and "the mountains" which follow, as literal mountains, as Dr. Baldwin seems to do, is to mar the consistency and harmony of the text.

The United States may occupy, literally, as Prof. Maury asserts, the highest part of the earth; and if so, it may be in allusion to this fact, that the nations are said to go up to it. But the hypothesis, whether true or not true, has nothing to do with the "mountains" here mentioned. These are, in accordance with sacred symbols, governments, and the meaning of the figure is, we think, that of one government established in the top of other governments. Israel restored is a federal nationality.

The federal character of the fifth kingdom is further manifest, from the fact that it is Israel restored. The ancient, peculiar people of God, was a collection of twelve; afterwards, of thirteen tribes. Their tribeship was far more obvious than their federative character. The former was essential; the latter, as found in the leadership of all the tribes by Moses and Joshua, was of a more incidental, and partial, and temporary character. So strongly was consolidation in their government resisted, that even after the reign of partial anarchy in the time of the Judges, the Almighty decided that the request of a king by his people was the rejection of himself as their ruler. The idea of Israel's nationality was that of many in one of the several equal tribes, with a visible center of unity under the common headship and control of Almighty God.

The federative character of the fifth kingdom is clearly discoverable in the vision of the Ancient of days. He is represented as coming when the thrones are cast down. Any one who has a Hebrew bible and lexicon, and is prepared to use them, can at once satisfy himself that the original word rendered "cast down," as truly means "set up, or erected." There can be no sort of doubt on this point.

Dr. Clarke, on this passage, says: "The word *Remayu* might be translated erected; so the Vulgate *positi sunt*, and so all the versions." Bishop Newton, in quoting the passage, renders "till the thrones were cast down" "*till the thrones were set up;*" and in the margin quotes the Vulgate, Septuagint, Syriac, and Arabic, as agreeing in this translation. He further says, the same word is used in the Chaldee paraphrase of Jer. 1:15; they shall *sit every one on his throne*. Matthew Henry says: "I beheld till the thrones were set up; so it might as well be read." Frey, a Hebrew, in his lexicon, translates *remayu* by *erecti sunt* — were erected. The Septuagint has *etethesan*, placed, the same in meaning with the term *positi* in the Vulgate So much for the question of philology here involved.

The movement of the thrones, whatever may be, is preparatory to the sitting of the Ancient of days. "I beheld till the thrones wet cast down, *and* the Ancient of days did sit." The present translation involves the apparent absurdity of saying that the thrones, or governments, are so alarmed at the very approach of the Ancient, as to fall before he could do anything to effect their overthrow. These thrones falling cannot mean the destruction of the little horn for that is one, and is destroyed in consequent of the action of the Ancient after his coming. cannot mean that the other "horns" of the bear fall, preparatory to the sitting of the Ancient.

The governments said to have fallen, are called "thrones," as distinguished from the "horns." If the Ancient had built up his dominion on the fallen "horns" undoubtedly it would have been stated, as in the case of the little horn, before which "three horns were plucked up," Beside, the "stone," and not the ancient or mountain, is said to have destroyed the empire, by breaking the feet of the image.

Nor can it be said, on the other hand, that any of these horns were set up as preparatory to the sitting of the Ancient of days; for these horns had appeared long before, and the little horn had long worn out the saints of the Most High.

In truth, it cannot be rationally said that any thrones, outside the Ancient's own territory, could possibly be either cast down or set up, preparatory to his coming. If the thrones included in his dominion were cast down, in order to his sitting, then he secures his high place like the beasts before him, by the subjugation of kingdoms; but this is contradicted by the entire character of the Ancient, as in contrast with the beasts. Besides, he cannot cast these thrones down, to extend his dominion, before he comes and sits, as here represented.

Further, the action of the thrones is to furnish a seat for the Ancient, which they could not do by falling to the ground; but by lifting themselves up in might and majesty to sustain him. The prophecy was realized when the thirteen colonies were "set up" as thrones, or sovereign and independent States, and as such, united to furnish a seat for the federal government of the United States. In this, we see a union of the thirteen tribes in the antitype, or "the mountain of the house of the Lord, established in the top, of the mountains."

Bishop Newton, Dr. Clarke, and others, think the scene here is that of a grand sanhedrin or council, with its president in the midst. The idea is beautifully appropriate. The Ancient takes his seat when the thrones are placed around, or "set up" for his reception. The federal government sits in the midst of the States, united with him in sending abroad the fiery stream of civil and religious freedom among the despotisms of the old world.

Dr. Baldwin has, in his Armageddon, elaborated and illustrated a very useful thought, that as ancient Israel contained the national and ecclesiastical departments, both essential to human nature and society, as such, the same is true of Israel restored; and that these two departments are distinctively symbolized, and that the symbols are in many instances repeated; thus furnishing four symbols: two for the one department and two for the other, just as Pharaoh's dream was repeated, to confirm its truth.

Dr. Clarke notices the same general thought, in his note on Zech. 4:14, in speaking of Zerubbabel and Joshua, as respectively symbolizing or representing the civil and ecclesiastical departments of Israel. We think we have found this to be true in the symbols of Israel restored.

Thus, in the vision of the Ancient of days, we have his name and venerable appearance signifying that he is an ancient government, reappearing, or Israel restored in antitype. The hoary head represents, further, honor, wisdom, superiority, etc. We have for the nationality, the Ancient himself; for the church idea or symbol, his government, which is white as snow. Linen, clean and white, is "the righteousness of the saints." The symbol denotes the purity of the church.

The symbols are repeated, and we have the Ancient's throne, which signifies government, or nationality. The "thrones" are set up, and by their union, form one throne for the Ancient, just as the mountains unite their tops as a base for the great mountain. This throne is a fiery flame, to denote the purity, energy, and strength of the nationality thus set up.

The church department is further expressed in the wheels of burning fire. Here, the image of fire, as indicating purity, energy, etc., in the government, is intensified. While the throne is of fiery flame, the wheels are of burning fire, as signifying the character of the christianity developed under the Ancient of days.

The Ancient and his throne being in motion, these wheels, denotes a rapidly expanding religion and nationality, over an extending population, in a wilderness country. Such has been the case. Population has extended from the already "inhabited parts of the country," over the land that had been always waste, and a pure christianity has gone with them, and the government has been extended over these settlements, first as territories, and then as States, resulting in a vast and glorious christian nationality, the wonder and admiration of the world.

CHAPTER V

THE CONFEDERATE STATES

The closing symbols represent the Confederate States —The stone cut out of the mountain—without hands—Isa. 66:7-8.—Isa. 4.— The mountain of the house of the Lord—The trouble of Zion — The seven women—Micah 4, 5.—The mountain of the house— The remnant—The first dominion—The birth of the Savior—Birth of the man child—Seven shepherds, and eight principal men—The war.

HAVING shown that the dream of Nebuchadnezzar, Dan. 2, and the first vision of Daniel, chap. 7, fully coincide in their respective six symbols; that they all represent civil governments, and that the fifth kingdom, symbolized by the mountain and the Ancient of days, is the United States, we come now to establish the identity of the closing symbols, the stone cut out of the mountain, and the one like the Son of man, with the Confederate States of America.

It may be asserted with entire confidence, that if the fifth kingdom be the United States, the sixth is, and must be, the Confederate States. The latter nationality was cut out of the former — out of the very body of the government; taking away the chief strength and support of the national greatness, and leaving the larger proportion of the territory behind; all which we understand to be indicated by the figure here employed. It was *cut,* not *torn* out — smoothly blocked away in the secession of the States as such, which, however, on account of the formation of a common government, as well as their perfect homogeneity in institutions, interest, and feeling, as well as political and commercial strength, are represented as a stone — as emphatically one stone.

The stone was cut out of the mountain *without hands,* or, as the margin reads, which was *not in hands.* The original *lo baidain* will bear either translation. In view of the marginal rendering, the phrase may be understood to mean that where no semblance, even, of separate government had existed, no reins of independent empire had been held by human hands, where the stone was simply part of and one with, the mountain, lo! suddenly, and to the amazement of the world, a mighty kingdom, even the final kingdom, arose. We consider the phrase as explained, however, by verse 44: "In the days of these kings shall *the God of heaven* set up a kingdom."

This notes the strictly providential — the Divine origin of the stone kingdom. But it signifies further, that the kingdom thus set up, is indeed God's kingdom, in which he will ever reign — from which he will radiate millennial glory over the earth.

The setting up of this kingdom, as a stone cut out of the mountain without hands, denotes the smallness of human effort and means actually employed in its erection. By a sudden, simultaneous, amazing impulse of the people, was the secession of the original seven States brought about, and by the like impulse, when additional momentum was given to the movement, did the other four States follow them.

If, as we understand, the Savior is to rule in the sixth kingdom, is not his language in Matt. 24:27, applicable to the manner of its rise? — "As the lightning cometh out of the east and shineth even unto the west, so shall also the coming of the Son of man be in his kingdom." Thus, with lightning swiftness, did the movement go from east to west, until the "seven" States were ready to form a common government.

This coming of the final kingdom, without observation or outward show, and without previous sufferings of a political redemption, is illustrated in Isaiah 65:7,8: "Before she travailed, she brought forth; before her pain came, she was delivered of a man child. Who hath heard such a thing? Who hath seen such things? Shall the earth be made to bring forth in one day, or shall a *nation, be born,* at once? for as soon as Zion travailed, she brought forth her children."

The same event styled the birth of "a man child," is also called the birth of "children ;" and this event, it is clearly intimated, is the birth of "a nation at once." The nation thus suddenly born, sustains the idea of many in one. In one sense, a man child; in another sense, many children. This birth occurred as soon, even before, the travail of Zion, or Israel, in the antitype. Thus, the nation did not arise out of the smoke and carnage of war; but, by a providential impulse of the people, was "born at once." The vision obviously refers to the future Zion. The event is followed by glory and joy of the "Jerusalem" in the final antitype. Verses 10-14 It will soon be seen that this birth was, in another sense, preceded by internal commotion and trouble. It is also declared in this passage, that in the enlarging dominions of the man child, other children will be born, besides the original ones, as has already been realized, and as the future will more fully reveal.

The mountain in the king's vision being, as we have seen, the mountain of the house of the Lord, established in the top of the mountains, or, as intimated, in the *name* and description of the Ancient of days, Israel restored in the antitype, or United States, we may expect to find in the prophecies relating to this mountain, a division answering to the cutting of the stone out of the mountain without hands.

Accordingly, the division of Israel, after its restoration, is just as clearly revealed with even, as we believe, the events of that division, as they have recently occurred, as that restoration itself. Israel chosen, and Israel divided, constituted the type. Israel restored, and Israel divided, as decisively constitute the antitype. When this event occurs, and not till then, the antitype becomes perfect.

Old Israel was divided, and while most of the tribes went into captivity, and were lost, Judah remained until after the coming of the Son of man. Israel restored is also divided, and while the majority of its tribes, or States, go into captivity, to the spirit of the old monarchies, a remnant is reserved, as the kingdom that shall never be moved.

The reader is now referred to Isaiah 2, 3, 4 in which the division, after the restoration, is intimated, though not so clearly and decisively, as in other places we shall notice. These chapters plainly constitute one connected prophecy. Such, too, is the view of Clarke, Scott, and others.

In the 2d verse, chap. 2r, we have the mountain of the

house of the Lord established in the top of the mountains, which, as synchronizing with the mountain in Nebuchadnezzar's vision, and with Israel restored, we have identified as the United States. We have in the succeeding verses, down to the fourth, inclusive, a glowing description of Israel restored, without special reference to the division, excepting that the 4th verse may more specially refer to the remnant after the division, as the grand instrument in bringing about millennial peace and glory; when "nation shall not lift up sword against nation, neither shall they learn war any more."

This identity of Israel, before and after division, is illustrated in the type, when the tribes that remained, after the loss of the others, retained the inheritance, as to emolument and promise, which had belonged to Israel as a whole, and constituted, indeed, the entire Israel of God.

The same is further illustrated by the obvious fact, that the stone partakes of, and concentrates the character of the mountain out of which it is taken, and inherits from it the final dominion. Thus, too, the one, like the Son of man, plainly agrees in spirit with the Ancient of days, and takes from him the kingdom; and thus, the man child directly succeeds his mother in the glorious inheritance.

As the typical Israel was one, notwithstanding the typical division, so the antitypical Israel is one, notwithstanding the antitypical division. As, however, the *fact* of the former division is recorded in history, so the fact of the latter division is, with sufficient clearness, revealed in prophecy.

On the passage under consideration, Bishop Lowth says: "There needs no other proof that the grand accomplishment of this prophecy is reserved to some future period, than the consideration that nothing in any measure answerable to such forcible expressions, has yet occurred on earth."

The former part of this prophecy, which relates to the establishment of the mountain of the house of the Lord, as the great center of human immigration, has been fulfilled, in the rise of the United States, and the remainder, however glorious, will be realized, when, after the great "time of trouble," which has now commenced, is over, millennial glory shall spread abroad, from the final remnant of Israel as its center, to the ends of the earth.

As the beginning of this great prophecy, contained in these three chapters, is future, so is the remainder of it future. And, after the above sublime outline, the prophet enters into details as to the division represented in the cutting of the stone out of the mountain.

In the 2d and 3d chapters, are presented the apostasies of the daughter of Zion. After setting forth in strong eastern phraseology, the crimes and follies, the wealth and power, the pride and haughtiness of her great controlling tribes, or States, the prophet describes in terrible language, the scenes of fear and dismay, of humiliation and ruin, which are to ensue. How fearful the destiny of the daughter of Zion!

Her mighty and her wise men are taken away; an idol shepherd is raised up; children are their princes, and babes of no understanding rule. Oppression becomes the order of the day, and the prophetic Jerusalem is ruined, and Judah is fallen. The crown of the head of the daughters, or tribes of Zion, is smitten with a scab, when the Lord shall enter into judgment with the ancients of his people.

In this day of terrible national judgment, which shall be upon the proud and lofty, the cedars of Lebanon, and the oaks of Bashan — the mountains and hills, the high tower, and the fenced wall, the ships of Tarshish and the pleasant pictures, or pictures of desire, men are exhorted to enter into the rock and hide in the dust, to go into the depths of the rocks, and the top of the ragged rocks, for fear of the Lord, and for the glory of his majesty, when he ariseth to shake terribly the earth.

The men of Zion shall fall by the sword, and her mighty in the war, and her gates shall lament and mourn, and she, being desolate, shall sit upon the ground. Isa. iii. 25, 26. How terrible is the doom of the great coercion States of the North, as presented in these, and numerous other prophecies, which shall come under review as we proceed!

"And in that day, seven women shall take hold of one man, saying, We will eat our own bread and wear our own apparel; only let us be called by thy name to take away our reproach. Isaiah 4:1.

Dr. Clarke thinks this verse refers to the slaughter mentioned in the last verses in the preceding chapter. But when will war be so destructive, as to leave but one-seventh of the men of a nation? Besides, the desire of the women is, that reproach shall be taken away from them. But is it a reproach to be the widow of a man slain in battle? And inasmuch as this is written of future times, the reproach of unmarried life and of destitution of children, felt among the ancient Jews, who constantly expected the birth of Messiah, must have passed away.

Further, when it is said, "In that day, seven women shall take hold of one man," it immediately succeeds that "In that day," i.e., the same day, the branch of the Lord is beautiful and glorious, and the fruit of the earth shall be excellent and comely for them that are escaped of Israel." Verse 3. The day of the movement of the women, and the day of the branch of the Lord, are thus seen to be the same day.

The two, therefore, coincide as to time. But the taking hold of one man by seven women, which, literally understood, would signify very great degradation in morals, would certainly be very distant from the scene of glory with which it is identified in the text. What can be the explanation? Simply, the following, as we fully believe:

In the parallel passage in Micah 5, the mountain of the house of the Lord, or Israel restored, is called the daughter of Zion, to whom comes the *first* dominion. This is the United States, as we have seen. In Isa. 3:16, we have the daughters of Zion, as many. These are the tribes, or States, of Israel restored, and rejected.

In contradistinction with these daughters of Zion, we have the seven women, or tribes, or States, who secede from the sisterhood of these proud and oppressive daughters. These women are poorer than those proud ones, as indicated in 3:15, and forsake the sisterhood of daughters, or States, to escape the oppression there stated.

One after another of these seven women, or States,

secedes. They are separate from each other, and from a hostile world. Driven out of the national Union, they are feeble women, helpless widows. After inheriting, with others, a national glory, preeminent in the world, will they be content with their isolated, feeble, reproachful condition? Not at all. But being united in their exile, and in interest and sympathies and feeling, they will seek a strong and glorious common nationality to take the place of the one they have forsaken.

The fulfillment of the passage is found in the seven seceding States forming the central government of the Confederate States. This is, as we shall see, the man child of the daughter of Zion. What is here said of the branch of the Lord, and of every one, i.e., every tribe that is left in Zion living, when others die, as to the covenant, coincides with what is elsewhere said of the "remnant" of Israel restored, and divided, and of the stone kingdom, and the one like unto the Son of man. We need not elaborate further, as many other more explicit passages will claim attention.

It may be added in this connection, however, that, as the ten horns of the fourth beast, as Sir Isaac Newton says, whatever their number afterwards, they are still called ten kings, from their first number, so the number seven, so often applied in the prophecies to the final kingdom, represents all the States that follow them; though these, too, are, in addition, expressly mentioned, and their number definitely given.

Attention is now invited to the fourth and fifth chapters of the book of Micah,

The concluding verse of the third chapter may be understood as referring to old Israel in the type: "Therefore shall Zion for your sake be ploughed as a field, and Jerusalem shall become heaps, and the mountain of the house as the high places of the forest." This verse shows the identity of Zion and Jerusalem with the mountain, or mountain of the house, both in the type and the antitype. Verses 1-3 of chap. 4, form an almost literal quotation from Isa. 2:2,3.

The exposition of that passage is applicable to this, with the exception that the general prophecy is here divided into two paragraphs; the former consisting of verses 1, 2, having special reference to Israel restored, or the United States; the latter, consisting of verses 3-5, having particular application to the remnant left after the division.

"In that day" referring to what immediately precedes, "saith the Lord, I will assemble her that halteth, and I will gather her that is driven out, and her that I have afflicted, and I will make her that halteth a remnant, and her that was cast far off a strong nation; and the Lord shall reign over them in mount Zion from henceforth, even for ever." (Verses 6, 7)

The remnant here mentioned, is plainly the remnant or portion of a people. It could not be the whole of the people referred to. Such an application of the term remnant would be absurd. The remnant must be a portion, and the smaller portion reserved when the larger part is cast off; and cast off because the remnant was cast off by this controlling majority.

The casting far off denotes a sectional separation wide and permanent. It does not mean a driving away to the ends of the earth into captivity. The fact that the remnant becomes a strong nation, and is under the direct control of the Lord of hosts, would forbid this interpretation. The remnant is said to become, under a Divine guidance, a *nation* — a strong nation.

The remnant was then a portion of the people; it is now separated, and becomes a strong nation under the reign of the Lord. This reign is perpetual, everlasting. The locality of this reign, is mount Zion. And this fact, together with that which precedes and which follows the text, signifies that this strong nation is the remnant of Israel restored in the last days.

This remnant — this strong nation, over which the Lord will reign for ever, is none other than the stone cut out of the mountain, or the one like the Son of man. They are positively identified by the same character of strength, and the same perpetual, everlasting reign of Almighty God.

This position is rendered more indubitably sure by the connection following, and by other passages to come under review. This division of Israel restored is yet more clearly exhibited 'under the figure of the birth of a man child.

"And thou, O tower of the flock! the stronghold of the daughter of Zion, unto thee it shall come, even the first dominion; the kingdom shall come to the daughter of Jerusalem." (Verse 8.) The tower of the flock is the central government for the oversight and protection of the restored Israel, or flock of the Lord.

The term stronghold signifies further, the strength and glory of the nationality represented as the daughter of Zion. Our Saviour declared to the literal Jews that the kingdom should be taken from them, and given to a nation bringing forth the fruits thereof. The fact that this kingdom is given to a *nation,* clearly shows that it is not a spiritual, but a civil kingdom; the Divine civil government of the Hebrew commonwealth revived in the antitype.

To Israel restored the mountain of the Lord's house established in the top of the mountains, or the United States, comes the *first dominion.* Not with the original old Zion, but with the daughter of Zion, the daughter of Jerusalem, is this first dominion, or first manifestation of the Divine kingdom in the antitype.

"Now why dost thou cry out aloud? is there no king in thee? is thy counselor perished?" One is almost ready to ask, Where are thy Clays and Calhouns and Websters? Where are the strong arms upon which thou hast leaned heretofore? Where are the great leaders to whom thou hast looked for guidance in times of distress and danger? Verily, the time of Zion's trouble is come. "For pangs have taken thee as a woman in travail. Be in pain, and labor to bring forth, O daughter of Zion, like a woman in travail: for now shalt thou go forth out of the city, and thou shalt dwell in the field, and there thou shalt be delivered; there shall the Lord redeem thee from the hand of thine enemies." (Verse 10.)

Though in the sudden birth of the new nationality there may truly be said to have been no preceding travail, in the way of war and carnage, the ordinary antecedents of a new government, yet in another sense Zion travailed before she brought forth. And every reader will at once realize the appropriateness of this expressive figure, in its application to the last several years of the history of the United States.

The city out of which the daughter of Zion goes, is determined by the whole connection, especially verse 8, to be Jerusalem in the antitype, so often spoken of by the prophets. This is inhabited after the departure of the daughter by her child, as heir to the inheritance, and styled in verse 7 the remnant, and the strong nation. The going out into the field, does not signify a local removal, but is the antithesis of the casting off of the remnant in verse 7. It is the same in meaning as to locality, with the promise, "I will remove far off the northern army." (Joel 2:20.)

This going out of Jerusalem, is a departure in spirit and principle, as we shall hereafter more clearly see from the covenant of Israel restored. Her going into the field signifies her exclusion from the shelter of God's protection and blessing, as his peculiar people. Her going even to Babylon, denotes so thorough a departure on the part of the daughter of Zion from her original condition as the Israel of God, as that she goes into captivity to the very opposite spirit and principle.

This is illustrated in the fact before referred to, that the stone, though cut out of the mountain *after* the *toes* of the image appear, yet strikes the feet of the image; denoting a reconstruction of the empire; a reconstruction in *spirit,* and without reference to locality and form. That the whole spirit and character of that series of empires is found in this reconstruction, is plain from the fact already stated, that the "brass, and silver, and gold, as well as the iron and clay," are found in the feet when stricken by the stone, (Dan. 2:35,); as also from the fact stated, (chap. 7:12,) that when the dominion of these great beasts is taken away, "their lives were prolonged for a season and a time."

The whole spirit of the old empires is found in the final conflict between liberty and despotism. And now we may appeal to the reader as to the application of this to the United States, since the rise of the Confederate States. Read the message of President Lincoln to the called session of Congress on the fourth of the present month, (July, 1861,) and look at the consolidated despotism arising on the destruction of the rights of States as such.

Note his attempted apologies for infractions of the Constitution, in the invasion of the dearest personal and social rights, and his call for four hundred thousand men and four hundred millions of dollars for the subjugation of the new nationality of the South. See how this has been responded to by the Congressional approbation of even an additional hundred thousand men, and a hundred million dollars more than required.

Consider also the participation of the spirit of the Government by the masses of the people. We ask then, is not the whole spirit of the old monarchies the spirit of despotism, of subjugation, and war, being rapidly developed in the United States, as one of the feet, thus to speak, of the image to be broken by the stone cut out of the mountain.

The history of this spirit of monarchy, in its conquest of Israel restored, is noted in the succeeding visions of Daniel. When it has prevailed, even in its more incipient stages in the government, the birth of this child of the daughter of Zion occurs. (Verse 10.)

The redemption of Zion, after his birth, from the hand of her enemies, may point out the identity of the daughter of Zion, in her original character, with her son, and her redemption in him as representing the remnant that is saved, or it may mean the revival of the spirit of the Constitution in some of the States of the North, as the 'Western or Pacific States, resulting in a great war, in which the government will be overthrown. The promise is true in either application, as shall appear hereafter.

The child that is born is determined, in chap. 5:4, to be a man child. His birth is also identified with that of *children,* as in Isa. 66 showing that he is one in one sense, and many in another sense, or many in one. It is also, as we believe, referred to in Jer. 15:9, as in the connection we are expounding, as the birth of seven, in allusion to the seven original States in the dominion of the man child, "She that hath borne seven languisheth: she hath given up the ghost; her sun is gone down while it was yet day." Alas, for the fate of the daughter of Zion. The day of her trouble, ay, of her death, as to the covenant of God's Israel, has come.

The time of the birth of this child of the daughter of Zion is fixed in chapter 5:1,2. "But thou Bethlehem Ephratah, though thou be little among the thousands of Judah, yet out of thee shall he come forth unto me that is to be ruler in Israel, whose goings forth have been from of old, even from everlasting." This is applied in Matt. 2:6, to the birth of the Divine Redeemer personally. He is here characterized as he *that is to Le* (hereafter) ruler in Israel, when Israel shall be restored as the final kingdom.

"Therefore will he, 'the Saviour,' give them up until the time that she which travaileth, hath brought forth. Then shall the remnant of his brethren return unto the children of Israel."

Those given up by our Saviour are his brethren after the flesh, the people among whom he was born. They are here distinguished from "the children of Israel," showing that Israel in the antitype is different from the literal old type.

The children of Israel are not the Church, as such, being plainly identified with the remnant that becomes a strong nation. v 7, and with the child of the daughter of Zion. It is said here that when this birth occurs, *then* the remnant of his brethren shall return to the children of Israel.

Thus the kingdom that, according to the Saviour's assertion, was to be taken from these literal brethren, has come as to its *first dominion* to the daughter of Zion, identified with the "mountain of the Lord's house," or the United States, and passes in its final dominion to her son, who synchronizes with the stone kingdom, or the Confederate States. It then finds a nation bringing forth the fruits thereof, as will more and more fully appear, as we believe, in the future history of the new nationality that has so suddenly and gloriously risen up in the world.

To his literal brethren our Saviour said, "Behold your house is left unto you desolate; and verily I say unto you, Ye shall not see me until the time come when ye shall say, Blessed is he that cometh in the name of the Lord." Luke 13:35. The time of his absence and their desolation is the period during which he is said, in the passage under consideration, to "give them up."

He that cometh in the name of the Lord is the child of the daughter of Zion, coming in the name of the Lord, and bearing his name, as the nationality in which he rules. Or if this phrase be applied to the Saviour himself, as in some passages in the Evangelists, then it is to him, as coming in the glory of his final reign, when the language of the multitude is specially appropriate: "Blessed is the king that cometh in the name of the Lord: peace in heaven and glory in the highest." Luke 19:38.

The Jews rejected him in his humiliation, and were "given up" to unbelief. The veil will remain upon their hearts until they see him in the glory of the final kingdom. Then shall the remnant of his brethren return unto the children of Israel.

The man' child of the daughter of Zion spoken of in the passage under discussion, is not born until after our Saviour's personal advent, nor until he has long given up his literal brethren, nor until near the time of their conversion, in which conversion he is said to be instrumental, as will doubtless be seen in the future. This period is, as the whole connection shows, that of the division of Israel restored, and the rise of the sixth kingdom, or Confederate States.

"And he shall stand and feed in the strength of the Lord, in the majesty of the name of the Lord his God; and they shall abide; for now shall he be great unto the ends of the earth. And this man shall be the peace when the Assyrian shall come into our land; and when he shall tread in our palaces then shall we raise against him seven shepherds and eight principal men," or, as the margin reads, "princes of men." v. 4, 5.

This passage cannot possibly refer literally, to the old Assyrian power. The unbroken connection in which it stands, places its fulfillment after the birth of our Savior, and even late in gospel times. The man who is to be our peace, must be the one just spoken of, as having been born.

The Assyrian power had passed away before the birth of our Savior, much more before the birth of the son of Zion, mentioned in verse 3. "Besides," as Scott says, "Senacherrib's invasion was not repelled by the rulers or chieftains of Israel; 2 Kings 19-35; nor did the Jews ever invade or waste the Assyrian dominions, or those of the Chaldeans, who afterwards occupied the same regions, it seems evident that these expressions must be understood as mystically intending other enemies of the church, who should be of the same spirit with Senacherrib and the Assyrians."

The whole connection shows that the oppressed people mentioned here, is the final "remnant of Israel restored, chap. 4:7, represented by the man child of the daughter of Zion, and that the Assyrian is the power attempting the subjugation of this remnant in the spirit of Senacherrib, and the Assyrians who invaded ancient Israel.

This is identical with the reconstructed Roman empire of the feet image, in which is found the gold of the head, or Assyrian empire, as well as all the other metals of the image. And other passages show that this final embodiment of the Assyrian spirit is found in Israel restored and rejected, and endeavoring to conquer the remnant.

He who is to be the peace, refers to the child of the daughter of Zion last spoken of, verse 3, with reference, too, to the personal Savior, who, as sitting on the right hand of power, reigns with the man child) and invisibly guides and sustains him in his dominion, according to the declaration in verse 2, "who is to be ruler in Israel."

Then shall we raise against him seven shepherds." The term "we" here refers to the remnant of Israel restored. The shepherds are the tribes of this remnant, in allusion to the occupation of the sons of Jacob, as the original heads of the tribes, and signifying, also, a very mild, beneficent sort of government. Seven shepherds and eight principal men, not meaning fifteen, but simply adding one to the seven, because of his importance, and as, perchance, representing another class.

The seven shepherds are tribes of the remnant of Israel restored, already under the peaceful dominion of the man child of Zion. The one added agrees in spirit with the shepherds, but does not occupy the same position with the shepherds. And yet, in another sense, he does occupy the same position; for though not numbered with the seven as shepherds, yet, when they are spoken of as princes of men, which phrase signifies government of some sort, he is numbered with them.

This enumeration, taking place in immediate connection with the invasion of the "Assyrian," signifies that the eighth is added partly, if not wholly, because of military power. The distinguishing of this eighth from the seven, and yet identification with them, seems to intimate that it is one of the tribes of Israel, not yet formally included in the remnant.

When the Government of the United States, as Israel restored, and rejected, had so far imbibed the Assyrian spirit as to undertake the subjugation of the remnant that had gone out, represented by the seven shepherds, or original Confederate States, the Convention of the State of Virginia at once adopted the ordinance of secession.

Vice-President Stephens was dispatched to confer with the Convention; and, in his message to the called session of Congress, President Davis announced that a Convention had been concluded, by which the vast military power of Virginia was added to that of the seven original States.

The action of Virginia, the great mother of States and of statesmen, is mentioned also by President Lincoln, in his message to Congress on the fourth of July, 1861, as exceedingly important.

The secession of Virginia was hailed with rapturous delight by the people of the seceded States, while it rendered the subjugation of the Confederate States even more certainly an impossibility. This great State is also a representative of the entire four, included in the second secession; all which are included, as we shall see in another passage, with the seven original States.

"And they shall waste (or eat up, as the margin reads,) the land of Assyria with the sword, and the land of Nimrod in the entrances thereof, (or, as the margin reads, with her on naked swords,) thus shall he deliver us from the Assyrian when he cometh into our land."

This land of Assyria is the same antitype of old "Assyria" above referred to, and we consider the passage as indicating that the Confederate States will be abundantly successful in resisting the power which seeks the overthrow of their independence.

If the marginal reading, "with her own naked, or unsheathed swords," be correct, and we do not insist upon it, then it points to a civil war in the North before the present scene of indignation and trouble shall have passed by. Whether this marginal rendering be admissible or not, we believe the passage to embrace this whole "time of trouble," and to receive illustration from the breaking of the feet of the image by the stone cut out of the mountain.

The people thus delivered, are the remnant of Jacob in the antitype, spoken of in verses 7, 8, and the succeeding part of the chapter.

The character of the government of this remnant is intimated. The term, "we will raise up," etc., must be applied to the people, and attributing to them great power, signifies a peoples' government. The seven shepherds are the tribe, or state government, the child of the daughter of Zion, who coincides with the remnant, and is the means of peace, by successfully resisting invasion in the Confederate government.

The connection of the Divine Redeemer with it, as ruler in Israel, shows that it is his Kingdom, in which he reigns, though invisibly. Thus it is written, "In that day shall the Lord be for a crown of glory, and for a diadem of beauty, unto the *residue* of his people. And for a spirit of judgment to him that sitteth in judgment; and for strength to them that turn the battle to the gate." That such has been the case with the Confederate States, as the "residue" of the restored Israel, or "people" of the Lord, we appeal to the reader for proof.

The great wisdom that has guided the government, and its amazing success in arms, have elicited attention and remark, not only in this country, but in Europe. That such will be the case hereafter, the prophecies, we believe, abundantly declare.

That this whole section of Micah's prophecy coincides with the visions of the mountain, and the stone cut of the mountain, and of the Ancient of days, and the one like the Son of man, is plain, not only from the details we have referred to, but from the fact that, substantially, the same things are said here of the "remnant of Jacob" that are stated as to the sixth kingdom in the visions.

CHAPTER VI
THE CONFEDERATE STATES—CONTINUED.

Zechariah's prophecies—Division of the Union—Border States as the slain shepherds—The eleven states as "the third"—The divided mountain—Ezek. 34. —The gathered flock judged and divided—Isa. 65:11-16—The Northern army—The American flag—Division —Contrast—One like the Son of man—Character of the government—How established—When it appears.

WE invite attention to some passages in the prophecies of Zechariah, in reference to the division of the restored Israel of God. The date of this book is placed from 520 to 500 B.C., about two hundred years after the division of Israel and Judah.

Zechariah is regarded as a very obscure prophet, not only in language and imagery, but as to the application and import of his predictions. The main reason why he is so hard to be understood, as we believe, is that he had more reference in his prophecies to Israel in the antitype than in the old type. And we are of opinion that, among other prophecies having reference to these latter times, he predicts, with sufficient distinctness, the division of the American Union as the modern Israel of God. This division is represented in chapter 11 under the idea of the breaking of two staves.

One staff is called Beauty, and represents the covenant between God and the people. The other is called Bands, and symbolizes the union of the tribes. "And I took my staff, even Beauty, and cut it asunder, that I might break my covenant which I had made with all the people." Zech. 11:10. "Then I cut asunder mine other staff, even Bands, that I might break the brotherhood between Judah and Israel." Verse 14. Archbishop Newcome says of this verse: "I cannot explain this passage without supposing that the kingdom of Israel subsisted when the prophet wrote it, and that either the wars between Judah and Israel are referred to, or the captivity of the ten tribes when the *brotherly connection* between these kingdoms ceased."

Dr. Clarke says, in the close of his notes on this chapter: "There are several things in this chapter that are very *obscure,* and we can hardly say what opinion is right, nor is it at all clear whether they refer to a very early or late period in Jewish history."

The great difficulty here is, that the prophet set forth in the breaking of the sticks the division of Israel, and yet he lived long after that division took place in the type. If, however, the transaction be referred to Israel in the anti-type, or the United States, it will be, as we think, more easily understood, especially in view of the memorable fact recorded in connection with it, in verses eighth and ninth:

"Three shepherds also I cut off in one month; and my soul loathed them, (or, as the margin reads, was straitened for them,) and their soul also abhorred me. Then said I, I will not feed you: that that dieth, let it die; and that that is to be cut off, let it be cut off; and let the rest eat every one the flesh of another."

The three shepherds, answering, though, in a different position, to the "seven shepherds," heretofore referred to, are three of the tribes of Israel restored. They are Maryland, Kentucky, and Missouri, for the present excluded from covenant of the final "Judah." They refused to come with the seceding States until the arm of federal power interposed to hold them back, as at this day.

They are "cut off" from the covenant of Judah, in contradistinction from the tribes of Israel that die as to the covenant, as signifying that they shall arise from the dust of the earth, when this time of trouble shall end in the overthrow of the power that oppresses them.

"Let the rest eat the flesh one of another." This points, as we believe, to the fearful conflict to take place among the States of the North, resulting in the three-fold division of their general government. Then, and not until then, will the slain shepherds arise. Not one of the border States will be able, as we believe, to enter the Southern Confederacy until that time. This opinion was expressed as early as the 13th of June, in the city of Houston, Texas, and is written here on the 31st day of July, 1861. This conclusion is based simply on this and other prophecies referring to these States.

This division is represented numerically as to the tribes or States, in chapter 13:7-9: "Awake, O sword, against my Shepherd, and against the man that is my fellow, (or, as Clarke renders it, 'upon the strong man,' or 'the hero that is with me,') saith the Lord of hosts: smite the shepherd, and the sheep shall be scattered; and I will turn mine hand upon the little ones. And it shall come to pass, that in all the land, saith the Lord, two parts therein shall be cut off and die; but the third shall be left therein. And I will bring the third part through the fire, and will refine them as silver is refined, and will try them as gold is tried: they shall call on my name, and I will hear them: I will say, It is my people; and they shall say, The Lord is my God."

The phrase, "smite the Shepherd, and the sheep shall be scattered," is quoted by our Saviour in application to his condition when his disciples all forsook him and fled. But this could not be the final fulfillment of the whole passage; for, instead of the fleeing of all the sheep, "two parts" are cut off and die, while "the third" remains.

Besides, the phrase "in all the land" decides the final fulfillment to be of a national character. If the prophecy be carried forward to the destruction of Jerusalem, is it true that two-thirds in all the land of Judea were then cut off and died? Is it true that the remaining third were brought through the fire and purified, and made the faithful servants of God?

This has assuredly not been realized in view of their persevering rejection of the Saviour, and, as we have seen, the veil will not be taken from their hearts until the fullness of the Gentiles is brought in, or the man child of the daughter of Zion, representing the final kingdom, appears, when they will return to the children of Israel.

We have seen that the whole passage cannot apply to the Saviour personally, and that it was not fulfilled in the destruction of Jerusalem. But if it be connected with the division of Israel restored, signified, as we have seen, by the breaking of the sticks or covenants, then the meaning is easy and plain.

The sword of Divine judgment smites the shepherd when the stick called Beauty is cut asunder, signifying that God's covenant with all the people, or Israel as a whole, is broken. "He thus shall accomplish to scatter the power of the holy people;" at the end and completion of prophetic vision, (see Dan. 12:7,) the passage under review is fulfilled.

Thus, when the United States Government, as the Ancient of days, is smitten, thirty-three States compose the Union. They are arranged in three classes: (1.) Those that *die* as to the covenant, as the coercion States of the North. (2.) Those that are cut off, as the three shepherds or border States; and the eleven Confederate States as "the third," which are even now being brought through the fire, in order to their purification: not as to their whole individual population, but as constituting the nationality of the final kingdom, in which the Lord rules.

In ch. 14:1-5, the division is represented geographically as to "the inhabited places of the country:" "Behold, the day of the Lord cometh, and thy spoil shall be divided in *the midst of thee.* For I will gather all nations against Jerusalem to battle." The term "earth" is in very numerous instances used for the land of Israel. See Symbolical Dic.

In a corresponding sense, the term nations or nations of the earth signifies simply the tribes or states of Israel restored. It was not true of the army of Titus, that it included all nations. But in the struggle which precipitated the fall of the Jerusalem of the prophets, or our Israel restored, all the classes of States — the aggressive States, the Southern States, those that promptly seceded, and those that did not—all in their several measures of policy contributed to this division. We need not enlarge here.

And "the city," or general government, shall be taken, and the "houses," or State governments, which are included in the city, rifled of their innocent, unaggressive character, and animated by the spirit of fratricidal war, and "the women," it may be churches, ravished of their innocence and purity, as to enter heartily into the war for the coercion and subjugation of the States of the South.

Thus, as we have seen, the Church idea is often presented in the prophecies of Israel restored, and such may be the meaning here. Now, whether we can hit the meaning in all the particulars or not, as it may be more a general than a particular description, we believe that the general idea of the conquest of Israel restored by the old monarchical principle, as set forth in other prophetic visions, to be involved here.

"And half of the city shall go forth into captivity." Allusion is had, in using the term "half," to the statement above: "Thy spoil shall be divided in the *midst* of thee;" and to the division of the mountain, when "half goes to the north and half to the south," including specially those States most thoroughly overcome by the despotic principle, now being rapidly developed in the United States Government. Thus it is written in Revelation, as we believe, in the same application, "He that leadeth into captivity shall go into captivity: he that killeth with the sword must be killed with the sword."

"Then shall the Lord go forth and fight against those nations," or States, "as he fought in the day of battle." He will interpose in giving aid to the arms of the residue, just as he did in the wars of his people in former times. The war is, in our judgment, the one now in progress. The amazing success at Great Bethel, Bull Run, Manassas, and indeed, throughout the war thus far, is a comment on this and kindred predictions.

Never, surely, since the wars of God's ancient people, has there been such remarkable and uniform success against such tremendous odds, and with such terror and dismay to the foe. The explanation is found in the fact that the Lord goes forth to fight against the coercion foes of his peculiar people. Thus it has been, and thus it will be to the close of the war.

"And his feet shall stand in that day upon the Mount of Olives, which is before Jerusalem, on the east, and the mount of Olives shall cleave in the midst thereof toward the East and toward the west, and there shall be a very great valley, and half of the mountain shall remove toward the north, and half of it toward the south. And ye shall flee to the valley of the mountains."

Our Saviour ascended from the literal Mount of Olives, and he shall stand on that mountain, or government, typified by the literal mount when he comes to reign. The Mount of Olives is here used as typical of the first dominion of Israel restored, or the mountain of the house of the Lord. This is, as we have seen, the United States.

When he thus stands on the mount, it divides asunder, half toward the north, and half of it toward the south. And the completeness of this division is signified by the great valley that intervenes, and by the fact that that valley lies now between two mountains which were parts of the same mountain. "And ye shall flee to the valley of the mountains," just as the border States have done, with the result shadowed forth in the figure of the three slain shepherds, which certainly accords with the facts as they now exist.

We have given what we doubt not is the true exposition of the text. The literal Mount of Olives cannot be referred to. Is it necessary to attempt to refute the supposition of Dr. Clarke that this text refers to the lines of circumvallation drawn by Titus in the siege of Jerusalem, represented as dividing the mount in twain, and forming a great valley between them? That interpretation was given because no other could then be found. The transaction is the cutting of the stone out of the mountain, and accordingly substantially the same things are said to follow the event here described, as are said of the stone kingdom in Dan. 2.

We have noticed only some of the main points in the remarkable prophecy of Zechariah, respecting the division of the modern Israel of God. We cannot now undertake to explain all the items contained in these chapters, though we believe that the whole connection is consistent with the exposition we have given. The prophecy coincides in meaning, as we doubt not, with numerous other predictions of the momentous events of these troublous times.

In further proof of the division of Israel in the antitype, we refer to Ezek. 34:12: "As a shepherd seeketh out his flock in the day that he is among his sheep that are scattered, so will I seek out my sheep, and will deliver them out of all places where they have been scattered in the cloudy and dark day, and I will bring them out from the people, and gather them from the countries and will bring them to their own land, and feed them upon the mountains of Israel, by the rivers, and in all the inhabited places of the country."

Here is the restoration of Israel in the antitype. There follows, however, a discrimination and judgment "between cattle and cattle," between one part of the flock and the other. The one is called the fat cattle, the other the lean cattle.

God expostulates with and reproaches the fat ones, thus: "Seemeth it a small thing unto you to have eaten up the good pasture, but ye must tread down with your feet the residue of your pastures, and to have drunk of the deep waters, but ye must foul the residue with your feet. And as for my flock, they eat that which ye have trodden with your feet, and they drink that which ye have fouled with your feet." Verses 18, 19. No illustration could more fully express the fact that the great Northern States have grown fat by the union, while, at the same time, abusing the poorer and weaker States of the South, which have, to a large extent, sustained and enriched them.

Addressing these fat and aggressive ones in favor of the lean ones, it is continued, "Behold I, even I, will judge between the fat cattle and between the lean cattle. Because ye have thrust with side and with shoulder, and pushed all the diseased with your horns, till ye have scattered them abroad, therefore will I save my flock, and they shall be no more a prey, and I will judge between cattle and cattle. And I will set up one shepherd over them, even my servant David: he shall feed them and he shall be their shepherd, and I the Lord will be their God, and my servant David a prince among them."

Here we have Israel restored in the glorious antitype, and a discrimination made between the fat cattle and the lean cattle. And while in this solemn judgment of the flock the former are cast off, the latter are saved as a remnant, and David in the antitype, or the Saviour, is set over them. A covenant of peace is established with them, and they are to be delivered from all "evil beasts," or oppressors. It is promised that they shall be a blessing, and that there shall be showers of blessing — that the tree of the field shall yield her fruit, and the earth shall yield her increase.

These and many other blessings are promised in the connection under consideration. A scene of peace and happiness and glory follows the division of the flock, and in connection with the remnant that is saved similar to that described of the stone, and the one like the son of man. In the one as in the others, we have the kingdom in which the Saviour rules.

Of the same import with the passages we have noticed is that contained in Isaiah 65:11-14: "But ye are they that forsake the Lord, that forget my holy mountain, that prepare a table for that troop, and furnish the drink-offering unto that number. Therefore will I number you to the sword, and ye shall all bow down to the slaughter: because when I called, ye did not answer; when I spake, ye did not hear; but did evil before mine eyes, and did choose that wherein I delighted not.

Therefore saith the Lord God, Behold, my servants shall eat, but ye shall be hungry: behold, my servants shall drink, but ye shall be thirsty: behold, my servants shall rejoice, but ye shall be ashamed: behold, my servants shall sing for joy of heart, but ye shall cry for sorrow of heart, and shall howl for vexation of spirit. And ye shall leave your name for a curse unto my chosen: for the Lord God shall slay thee, and call his servants by another name."

That those addressed here had belonged to the Israel of God, is plain from the fact that they are rebuked for forgetting him, and forsaking his holy mountain. That they had been called by the same name with the "servants" mentioned, is plain from the fact that these latter are now to be called by another name. The scene is laid, as the connection shows, in common with most of the prophecies of

Isaiah, in the latter times.

And here is the vision of the restored Israel, followed by a scene of glory that we have found elsewhere. Here is presented a striking contrast between those rebuked and cast off, represented by Ezekiel as the fat cattle, and those styled the Lord's servants or chosen, over whom he will reign. That contrast between the old nationality and the new has already commenced, and it will undoubtedly widen with the flight of months and years.

Those cast off are specially reproached, as preparing "a table for that troop," and as furnishing "the drink offering for that number." The troop is the great coercion army attempting the subjugation of the States of the South, which as being sustained at enormous expense, renders mention of the preparing of a table for it the more impressive.

A note in Bagster's Bible says, that "an infinite number of dissertations" have been written on "that number," *(meni,)* mentioned here as an object of idolatrous regard; and after stating the utter fruitlessness of all inquiry on the subject, significantly asks among other questions, Is it a number of stars here meant? We answer, It is we believe, the number of thirty four stars emblazoned on the American flag, and to which extraordinary honors have been paid.

A divine of the North, recently said in a grave religious convention, "We almost worship the flag." This witness is true. It has been suspended across the streets of towns and cities — has floated from the tops of private houses and public buildings, and even the temples of religious worship. It has been, it is said, in some instances — few we trust — even spread upon the communion table.

The "drink-offering of blood," to use the language of the Psalmist, has been poured out in its honor. How many have perished in sustaining that flag, even as the symbol of oppression and fratricidal war!

The Ancient of days is employed by the Almighty in judging European despotism, and particularly the Papal power. The sitting of this judgment is, as we have seen, according to some writers, taken from the grand sanhedrin, with its president, representing the Federal Government, and the consistory sitting around, all united in the deliberation and sentence of judgment. At the close of the probationary period involved in "the first dominion" of Israel restored, the tribes themselves are judged, as to their covenant of loyalty to God and his word, and of equality kindness, and justice, among themselves.

Those tribes that forsake God and forget his holy mountain, are as seen in the quotation from Isaiah, already examined, cast off. The other tribes as a remnant, retain the covenant blessings of God's peculiar people, and inherit the final glorious kingdom.

Among the reasons for this casting off, are their forsaking God — substituting opinion and sentiment for Divine authority; and the coercion war, it would seem, seals the sentence of exclusion from the heritage of God. They are specially reproached with the feeding of that troop, and thus making war upon their sister States.

Cast off, they go into captivity to the old monarchical principle. Endeavoring to subjugate others, they are subjugated themselves. And their central government, built upon the destruction of the rights of States, becomes indeed, in part at least, the reorganized Roman empire. Thus in the king's vision, it is to be inferred that the stone is cut out of the mountain, because of a change in the character of the mountain.

And we think that it will be found to be true, that in every other prophetic vision in which the Roman empire is found, its final exploit is the conquest of the holy land in the anti-type, or the destruction of the "mighty and holy people." But we cannot, however, discuss the subject in this connection.

"I saw in the night visions, and, behold, *one* like the Son of man came with the clouds of heaven, and came to the Ancient of days, and they brought him near before him." Dan. 7:13.

The one like the Son of man is certainly the stone cut out of the mountain. it is the opposite of the beasts preceding it, and is the highest ideal of free government, in spirit and in form. It is a glorious, powerful, christian republic.

It is also like the mountain, or Ancient of days—a federal republic. This is as certainly true of the stone, as of the mountain out of which it is taken. If the mountain be composed of States, the stone, which is part of it, must be composed of some of these States.

Thus, in Daniel's vision, the one like the Son of man comes to the Ancient of days to signify that, in spirit, he agrees with him, receives the kingdom from him, and is really the Ancient of days, or Israel finally restored in the antitype.

"And *they* brought him before him," i.e., before the Ancient of days. The term "they" agrees, in sense, with the saints of the Most High, mentioned in verse 18. "But the saints of the Most High shall take the kingdom, and possess the kingdom for ever, even for ever and ever."

It will be observed that the same preeminent, universal, and everlasting dominion attributed to the one like the Son of man is, in verse 18, ascribed to the saints of the Most High. These saints are, according to Dr. Clarke, *supreme, holy ones*; or, as Bishop Newton styles them, *holy ones*.

These supreme saints can hardly be considered in their personal character as taking the kingdom, or as bringing the one like the Son of man before the Ancient of days. If individual saints be meant in the word *kaddishai* here used, their governmental action must be had in organized form. But a man is often used as a symbol of government. Thus, the four successive monarchies are together embodied in the image of a man,

The ancient people of God were called Israel, the name of their father. The *tribe* of Judah is called Judah; and in the Revelation, the men who worship the beast and his image are, as we believe, not individual men, but states, or governments.

A *saint,* as a symbol of government, would represent a very mild, unoppressive christian rule. If, then, the word represents them individually, they must be embodied, in order to take the kingdom. And if the term *saints,* or *holy ones,* be used in a symbolic sense, as signifying governments, the same is true.

These saints, as a portion of Israel restored, are the "remnant" tribes spoken of elsewhere. Thus, in ancient times, Israel acted by tribes. It is predicted of the restoration in christian times, "Thou shall be gathered *one by one,* O! Israel." Thus, cooperation of the States utterly failed, in both the first and second secessions; and every State, or tribe, acted in accordance with the prophecy, by and for itself.

Thus, too, in the judgment of the tribes, when, as in Ezekiel, God is represented as judging between one part of the flock and the other, they must stand alone, just as in the final personal judgment, every one of us must give account of himself unto God. It would be entirely absurd to understand the prophecy literally, that the Jews will be gathered, one by one, individually, to their land.

Those coming, one by one, are the tribes, or States, in the final restoration. The tribes acting one by one form a central government. The one like the Son of man, is thus many in one — a king with many crowns — a glorious federative republic. The one like the Son of man is brought near before the Ancient. He is thus seen as agreeing with him in spirit.

Embodying now the whole spirit of Israel restored, he succeeds to the entire inheritance, and receives the supreme dominion. The Ancient, as synchronizing with the mountain, the daughter of Zion, or Israel restored, receives the "first dominion," or embodiment of the kingdom taken from the Jews, as the type. The one like the Son of man, agreeing with the stone cut out of the mountain, the man child of the daughter of Zion, the remnant, after the division of Israel, receives "dominion, and glory, and a kingdom, that all people, nations, and languages, should serve him. His dominion is an everlasting dominion, which shall not pass away, and his kingdom that which shall not be destroyed." Dan. 7:14.

As in the representations of Israel restored, we generally

have the ideas of the state and of the church, so in this final symbol. The one like the Son of man is the civil department of the final Israel; the clouds of heaven, with which he comes, represent the ecclesiastical department.

The term *clouds,* as being plural, signifies division in this latter department, and represents the churches existing in the final government at the time of its rise. Thus, our Saviour comes "sitting on the right hand of power, with the clouds of heaven." The "clouds of heaven" are the churches, the power, the civil government, and the Saviour sits on the right hand of this power, as "the spirit of judgment unto him that sitteth in judgment, and the spirit of strength unto them that turn the battle to the gates."

What is the time of the rise of the final kingdom? In the prophecies of Micah, which we have referred to, the man child of the daughter of Zion, or the restored Israel, is born, when she has passed under the control of the Babylonish spirit. In the passage from Ezekiel, the remnant of the flock is saved, when the judgment of the flock "between the fat cattle and the lean cattle" takes place.

Accordingly, in the vision of the Ancient of days, the judgment sits, and the books are opened. One of the books is the book of life for the tribes themselves. Thus, in Isaiah, at the time of the taking hold of one man by seven women, when the branch of the Lord shall be glorious, it is said that "he that is left in Zion, and he that remaineth in Jerusalem, shall be called holy, even every one that is *written* among the *living* in Jerusalem," — the living tribes, when the others die, as to the covenant of Israel.

Thus the angel said to Daniel, in reference to the time of trouble, which has now commenced, that "thy people shall be delivered, even every one that shall be found written in the book." Thus, there is a book of life for the final Israel, in the great national judgment, just as there is to be in the final personal judgment.

At this judgment, some of the tribes, or States, are cast of, and others reserved in the final kingdom. This is the scattering of the power of the holy people, spoken of in Daniel

12:7: "It shall be for a time, times, and a half; and when he shall have accomplished to scatter the power of the holy people, all these things shall be finished."

It is also stated, Dan. 7:25-26, that they, the saints, "shall be given into his hand," (that of the little horn) "until a time and times and the dividing of time. But the judgment shall sit, and they shall take away his dominion to consume and to destroy it unto the end." Now the end, in the latter verse, is the time when the mystery is finished.

Thus the scattering of the power of the holy people, and the destruction of the little horn, agree as to time. Now, the judgment begins, as to the little horn, when the Ancient comes, and his destruction progresses to the end. See verses 21, 22, 25, 26. The event, as to the holy people, let it be noted, is not the gathering, but the scattering of their power.

It is not the restoration of Israel, but the division of Israel. "When he shall have accomplished to *scatter* the power of the holy people, all these things shall be finished." As when Israel is thus divided, the remnant of the tribes that remain among the living, constitute, as we have seen, the final kingdom, it follows that the rise of that kingdom is at the "end." Thus the three events agree in time: the destruction of the little horn, the scattering of the power of the holy people, and the rise of the final kingdom. All these occur too, at the close of the great prophetic periods.

According to the understanding of many interpreters of prophecy, these prophetic periods cannot be far from their close. Within the past few months the three events have transpired which mark the end. The power of the little horn has been broken in the absorption of the States of the Church in the united kingdom of Italy. "The power of the holy people," called in chap. 8:24, "the mighty and the holy people," has been scattered, and the one like the Son of man has appeared in the rise of the Confederate States of America.

THE CONCLUSION

Philosophy of our theory—The book of Revelation—The time of trouble—Convulsions in Europe—Fall of the United States—The present war—Five months —Our national fast—Battle of Manassas—Breaking the blockade—National resurrection—The millennium—The final judgment—Heaven.

THE great moral fact which underlies the theory we advocate in this work is, that as Satan has been the god of this world, the prince of the power of the air, the controlling spirit in human government, he is to be conquered on that field, as well as on every other, by the Divine Redeemer.

Our Saviour had reference, as we believe, to this victory, when he rejoiced in spirit on seeing Satan fall as lightning from heaven. When this grand achievement is made, the prophetic vision is unsealed. The scene which introduces the national, or political prophecies of the book of Revelation is, we believe, simply a duplicate, under different symbols, of the Ancient of days, and the one like the Son of man.

The latter is here presented as the Lamb having seven horns and seven eyes, or the Saviour revealed in civil government. That is the government under which we live. The time of trouble, spoken of by Daniel the prophet, has, we believe, come, when every one, i.e., every tribe of our Israel, written in the book, shall be delivered, and included in the final kingdom.

There is, and will be, a mighty shaking of the heaven and the earth. The conflict will go on until, in Europe and America, despotism is effectually diminished, or overthrown, and oppressed nationalities shall be liberated from their thralldom. We would not speak with the confidence of a prophet; but if we have ascertained our present stand-point, we think it not irrational that some indications should be furnished, as to the general events of the future. We can but believe that very soon terrible convulsions will occur in Europe, in which despotism, though it may be at first triumphant, will be defeated, in the deliverance of nations now oppressed.

The time of trouble will, we believe, continue in the New World, until the rising despotism of the North shall be broken in pieces, and the slain shepherds, or border States, shall live again.

We understand this to be meant by the division of "the great city" into "three parts," (Rev. 16:19,) though we cannot now give the reasons for that opinion. How long it will be before this shall occur, we cannot tell. From intimations which we have, as we think, gathered in the prophecies, it will occur in a very few years.

The Confederate States will take part in the conflict which will overthrow that government. We cannot believe, however, that actual war will exist during all the intervening time. The present war is, as we doubt not, alluded to in many of the prophecies, especially in Joel 2, and in the fifth trumpet, Rev. 9.

The imagery employed is, in both cases, the same, and in both is noted the reflex influence of the war, and those engaged in pushing it forward. We understand the "torment," which "was as the torment of a scorpion when it stingeth a man," as describing the furious, unparalleled war spirit which has prevailed in the Northern States. This is said to continue five months.

We understand the book of Revelation, as the prophecies generally, to have an accommodated meaning, and a full, final application. The prophetic periods have also a symbolic, and finally, a literal meaning. And we think we have found events corresponding to the literal periods. The period given may, however, accord with a different reckoning of time from ours, or may embrace a more general length of time than that indicated. This idea of general, rather than specific periods, is entertained by some writers on prophecy.

Five months, as indicating the continuance of the war spirit in the North, would literally embrace the period intervening between the middle of April and the middle of September. About the latter period, it was found so difficult to procure soldiers for the Northern armies, that the system of drafting was urged as a matter of necessity.

The policy seemed to be generally advocated by the war journals of the North, of attacking the Atlantic and Gulf States by sea, while maintaining a defensive position on land, as the only hope of success in the war.

On the 26th of September was published in Richmond, and on yesterday, 29th, in Nashville, this intelligence: "The war feeling in the North seems to have generally subsided." If this be true, and we believe it is, the fact may have an important bearing on the future of the war.

It would not necessarily follow, from this effectual waning of the war spirit, preparatory to its final extinction, that the actual fighting would immediately cease. It may be five months, or even more, from the time that actual hostilities commenced, after the mighty uprising of the North, just alluded to, and their actual cessation.

The war is a "blast of the terrible ones against the wall," which wall is not, however, unshaken. It is promised, in application, as we believe, to this very case, that the Lord will go with the whirlwinds of the South, as he manifestly has done, and will do, to the end.

The exhortation in Joel, on the occurrence of this war is, that we should "blow the trumpet in Zion, sanctify a fast, call a solemn assembly." The fast was proclaimed, and proved to be the most solemn and universally observed one of modern times. Throughout all these States, men in the church and out of it, religious and irreligious, forsook their secular employments to mingle in the solemn public worship of Almighty God.

That day is referred to, as we believe, in Zech. 3:9: "For behold the stone that I have laid before Joshua; upon one stone shall be seven eyes: behold, I will engrave the graving thereof, saith the Lord of hosts, and I will remove the iniquity of that land in one day."

That the stone is an emblem of a nationality is plain, from

the mention of "that land." The seven eyes are in allusion to the seven original States, so often mentioned in these prophecies.

The removal, not of individual, but of national sins, is promised: "I will remove the iniquity of that land." This is to be done on a certain day, surely; a day of national humiliation and prayer. The verse was read on our national fast day, June 13th, and applied to that day. We still believe that the application was just. Does not the bestowment upon us of so many national blessings indicate this removal of national iniquity?

The result is further stated in Joel 2:18: "Then will the Lord be jealous for his land, and pity his people. Yea, the Lord will answer and say unto his people, Behold, I will send you corn, and wine, and oil, and ye shall be satisfied therewith: and I will no more make you a reproach among the heathen."

Has not the Lord pitied us? Has he not filled our land with plenty? Have we not heretofore been the reproach of the heathen, or as Ezekiel expressed it, "taken up in the lips of talkers"? The term heathen is used, as we think, in many places, of the tribes or States of Israel rejected.

"But I will remove far off from you the Northern army, and will drive him into a land barren and desolate, with his face toward the east sea, and his hinder part toward the utmost sea, and his stink shall come up, and his ill savor shall come up, because he hath done (or as the margin reads, magnified to do) great things."

When did an army "magnify to do" such "great things" as did the Northern army? Is the fact that so many bodies were left unburied on the various battle-fields of the present struggle, loading the atmosphere with pestilential stench, no illustration of this passage? The desolate state of the land is explained by the phrase used by Isaiah: "There shall be a great forsaking in the midst of the land."

If the theory we advocate be correct, then there is a general opening of the prophetic vision at the rise of the final kingdom. The Lamb with the seven horns opens the seals which, as is stated in Dan. 7:26; 12:4, 9, could not be opened till the time of the end, or the expiration of the prophetic periods. If this be so, then the prophecies generally are more applicable to these and succeeding times, than to those in which they were written.

The glorious Psalms too, many of which are allowed on all hands to be prophetic, contain very much that is more fully applicable to the final Zion of God, than to the literal old type. Take for example the 48th Psalm. Was this exclusively, or even mainly, applicable 'to the literal Jerusalem? Of this it was predicted that it should be "ploughed as a field," and "become heaps." See Mich. 3:12. Of the one in this Psalm it is said, "God will establish it for ever." This is just what is stated as to the perpetuity of the stone kingdom as the final Zion.

We invite attention to verses 3, 6. This passage was read on the 13th day of June last, and the opinion was then expressed that it would be fulfilled during the session of the Northern Congress, to assemble on the fourth of the succeeding month.

How was it fulfilled, "For, lo, the kings" (or rulers, or lawgivers, see Psa. 2:2,) were assembled, they passed by together," or went beyond the place of their assembling. "They saw it, and so they marveled," — they saw something for which they were not prepared, expecting victory but witnessing overwhelming defeat. "They were troubled and hasted away. Fear took hold upon them *there*" — i.e., at the place to which they went when they passed by together — "and pain as of a woman in travail" — extreme terror and dread producing intense desire to hasten away.

We believe this to be the terrible route of Manassas Plains, which was the more memorable as it included so many of the rulers and chief men of the North. Thus, in almost all the descriptions of that terrible scene, you have the flight of these same Congressmen alluded to, together with their great anxiety to hasten away.

"Thou breakest the ships of Tarshish" (which name may be appropriately used of any naval power) "with an east wind." This we believed then, and believe now, to have reference to the breaking of our blockade by a power or influence from the east, as of England and France. When this war shall have become history, we believe that the two decisive points in it will be, the battle of Manassas Plains and the breaking of the blockade. The great battle of the struggle has been fought, and the other decisive event will occur in due time.

"As we have heard, so have we seen in the city of the Lord of hosts, in the city of our God." Just as we have heard and read of God's dealings with his ancient Zion, so have we seen in its final antitype. Such are precisely the reflections and expressions of very many of our people now.

There are comparatively few intelligent and thoughtful men in the Confederate States, who do not acknowledge the hand of God in the battles that have been fought, and especially in that of Manassas Plains. And when the blockade shall have been broken by a power from the east, and the war terminated, as we believe it will be, without the sorrows of a terrible political redemption, the impression as to Divine interposition will be deeper and more all–pervading.

And whether we entertain any special views as to the destiny of the new nationality or not, we should, as a people, gratefully acknowledge the hand of God and devote ourselves to his service. "The Lord hath done great things for us, whereof we are glad."

When this time of trouble shall result in the downfall of overshadowing despotisms, and the resurrection of oppressed States and nationalities, we believe that the chaining of Satan as the ruling power in human despotism, in connection with the diminution of his power over mankind generally, will occur when civil liberty and pure Christianity will go abroad over the earth.

During the whole millennial period of glorious Christian triumph, the new nationality, as the highest ideal of human government and as under the control of the Saviour of the world, will stand central and preeminent among the nations of the earth. The King with many crowns, or the Saviour revealed in human civil government, will rule the nations with a "rod of iron," which signifies, we believe, the commerce of the world. He smites the nations with a sword, but one that "proceeds out of his mouth" — the doctrine of the purest civil and religious liberty, preached in his precepts and illustrated by his example.

In illustration of these items, we have the fact that the new nationality contains, or surrounds the fountain-head of human commerce, and that it possesses, as to outline, at least, the highest ideal of human government.

When the thousand years of the peaceful millennial reign shall be over, a short decisive conflict will ensue — after which the personal resurrection and final judgment. The earth will be renewed by fire: there will be no more sea. Then the stone cut of the mountain shall become a great mountain and fill the whole earth.

The confederate "nations of them that are saved "shall dwell on the renewed earth, under the direct reign of God for ever. There shall be no more curse nor "death, nor sorrow, nor crying." There shall be fullness of joy and pleasures for evermore.

We solemnly believe that the great prophetic periods have closed: the mystery is finished and the vision of prophecy is unsealed. The final kingdom has arisen, and the Divine Redeemer has come to reign. "Cry out thou inhabitant of Zion, for great is the Holy One in the midst of thee."

THE END

Various Books Published By
CONFEDERATE STATES PRINTING OFFICE[8]

You can find these fine books and others by C.S. Publishing Office at your favorite Bookseller, or at www.lulu.com

The Confederate States of America in Prophecy, by Rev. W.H. Seat, a Southern Methodist Minister, and is edited by Dr. William G. Peters. This work examines Daniel's prophecy of the of the Five Governments; with the United States as the Fifth Government and the Confederate States as the little stone cut from the mountain, as a revived Government of Judah.

The Eschatology of the United States as Restored Israel, and the Confederate States as a Restored Judah, is a secular prophecy of the people of North America as God's special chosen people.

In the heady days of Southern victories over Northern armies, Rev. Seat posits the future history of the Confederate States based upon the Prophet Daniel.

Sermons of the Confederacy 1861-1862, edited by Dr. William G. Peters, is a collection of sermons by Southern ministers, bishops, and priests, from 1861-1862.

These ministers cover, in their sermons and discourses, a wide range of subjects, from the cause of the War, differences between Yankees and Southerners, Negroes and their purpose among Southerners, the life and death of Confederate heroes, service to God, military service and Christian Faith, etc.

This is an excellent book for those who want to understand our Confederate ancestors, the C.S.A., and the South's Faith in God and victory in the face of implacable Northern invasion.

Sermons of the Confederacy 1863-1865, edited by Dr. William G. Peters, is a collection of sermons by Southern ministers, bishops, priests, and rabbi from 1863-1865, and a continuation from "Sermons of the Confederacy 1861-1862."

These men of God cover a wide range of subjects, from the cause of the War, differences between Yankees and Southerners, Negroes and their purpose among Southerners, the life and death of Confederate heroes, service to God, military service and Christian Faith, etc.

This is an excellent book for those who want to understand our Confederate ancestors, the C.S.A., and the South's Faith in God and victory in the face of death and destruction from Federal invasion.

---

[8] Also designated as C.S. Printing Office. A division of Confederate States of America, Inc.

The True Church Indicated to the Inquirer, by Bishop John McGill. Confederate Bishop of Richmond, Virginia, edited by Dr. William G. Peters.

Bp. McGill examines the claims of various and sundry groups to be the true Church. He examines these claims in the light of scripture, history, tradition and reason. Then he contrasts them against the claims of the Catholic Church to be the One, True Church, showing how the claims of all other groups fall short.

The Confederate Army Navy Prayer Book is the Episcopal Prayer Book for the Armed Services of the Confederacy. It went through annual editions from 1861-1865, and was the official prayer book of the Confederate States.

Additional prayers have been included, including national calls to prayer by President Jefferson Davis throughout the War, and a sermon by Bp. Stephen Elliot delivered upon the Day of National Humiliation, Fasting and Prayer in 1861.

The Catholic Devotional for Confederate Soldiers was written by Bishop McGill for the Confederate Soldier's to carry with them into battle, and for their encampments.

The work was published and registered by Bp. McGill in the Confederate States of America in 1861.

The Devotional contains many Catholic prayers, novenas, selections from the Mass, etc., which are appropriate to Catholics of all stripes.

Faith The Victory by Bishop John McGill, Confederate Bishop of Richmond, Virginia, edited by Dr. William G. Peters.

Bp. McGill presents an explanation of Catholic doctrine for Catholics and non-Catholics who hold to the old orthodox Protestant beliefs and traditions, and want to know more about the development and meaning of Christian doctrine.

A non-polemical work, the Bishop provides a rational explanation of sometimes difficult subjects. It is a clear concise summary of doctrinal points of interest to all Christians, without being either too brief, or tedious.

www.ingramcontent.com/pod-product-compliance
Lightning Source LLC
Chambersburg PA
CBHW020016050426
42450CB00005B/500